ASIAN NOODLES

86 Classic Recipes
from Vietnam, Thailand,
China, Korea and Japan

MAKI WATANABE

TUTTLE Publishing

Tokyo | Rutland, Vermont | Singapore

Contents

Foreword by Maki Watanabe 4
Asian Noodles Used in This Book 6
Flavorings and Spices Used in This Book 7
Toppings and Condiments to Go with Noodles 8

PART 1
Tossed or Mixed Noodles

TOSSED NOODLES CAN BE ENJOYED AS A SNACK OR A MEAL!

How to Boil Fresh Chinese Noodles 12
How to Boil Dried Chinese Noodles 13
Beijing-Style Pork Noodles with Black Bean Sauce 14
Sichuan Steamed Chicken with Noodles 15
Sliced Pork and Green Onion Noodles 16
Pork and Black Vinegar Chilled Noodles 17
Canton-Style Crispy Shrimp and Pork Noodles 18
Crab Omelette Crispy Noodles 19
Five-Spice Pork Noodles 20
Taiwanese Chicken Noodles 21
Simple Sesame and Green Onion Noodles 22
Dried Shrimp and Black Bean Sauce Noodles 22

Braised Soy Pork Noodles 23
Dry Tom Yum Noodles 24
Beef & Coriander Glass Noodles 24
Thai Rice Noodles with Pork and Spinach 25
Squid and Lemongrass Noodles with Peanut Sauce 26
Vietnamese River Noodles with Pork and Shrimp 26
Vietnamese Rice Noodles with Meatballs 27
Spicy Cold Korean Buckwheat Noodles 28
Korean Raw Fish and Perilla Buckwheat Noodles 28
How to Cook Japanese Noodles 29
Somen Noodles with Eggplant and Grated Daikon 31
Somen with Walnut Sauce 31
Warm Somen with Seaweed and Sour Plum Sauce 32
Warm Pork and Soy Milk Somen 32
Udon Salad with Tomatoes and Green Shiso 34
Chilled Curry Udon 34
Beef Udon 35
Yuba and Shirasu Udon 35

PART 2
Stir-Fried and Pan-Fried Noodles

GOING FROM STALL TO STALL ENJOYING STIR-FRIED NOODLES ON MY TRAVELS!

How to Stir Fry Mi Fun (Rice Vermicelli) 38
How to Stir Fry Precooked Chinese Noodles 39
Stir-Fried Mi Fun with Lots of Vegetables 40
Spicy Stir-Fried Mi Fun with Gochujang 41
Seafood Stir-Fried Mi Fun with Fresh Clams 42
Stir-Fried Mi Fun with Ground Pork and Bean Sprouts 43
Shanghainese Stir-Fried Noodles with Pork and Vegetables 44
Stir-Fried Ramen with Chives, Ginger and Scallops 45
Shanghai-Style Hot Sauce Noodles 46
Bean Sprout and Zha Cai Stir-Fried Noodles 47
Stir-Fried Glass Noodles with Scallops and Eggs 48
Stir-Fried Noodles with Water Spinach & Fish Sauce 48

Pad Thai with Shrimp 49
Vietnamese Stir-Fried Beef Noodles 50
Vietnamese Rice Noodles (Bun) with Beef and
    Basil 51
Korean Stir-Fried Glass Noodles with Beef Ribs 51
Stir-Fried Noodles with Kimchi and Dried Fish 52
Shrimp Roe Noodles 52
Stir-Fried Noodles with Bamboo Shoots, Pork and
    Oyster Sauce 53

PART 3

Soup Noodles

**EVERYONE LOVES A COMFORTING BOWL OF
    SOUP NOODLES**

How to Cook Rice Noodles 56
**How to Cook Mung Bean Glass or Cellophane
    Noodles** 57
Beef Pho Noodle Soup 58
Seafood Pho Noodle Soup 59
Chicken Pho Noodle Soup 60
Vegetable Pho Noodle Soup 61
Thai Curry Noodle Soup 62
Thai Lemongrass Noodles with Spare Ribs 63
Rich Bone Shank Pho 64
Shrimp Tom Yum 64
Thai-style Ramen with Pork and Crispy Wontons 65
Vietnamese Fried Fish Rice Noodle Soup 66
Vietnamese Chicken Glass Noodle Soup 67
Chilled Soba Noodle Soup with Shrimp Tempura 69
Chilled Soba with Okra and Mountain Yam 69
Hot and Sour Noodle Soup 70
Minced Pork Noodle Soup 71
Fish Ball and Celery Noodle Soup 72
Ramen with Beef and Tomato Soup 73
Fresh Clam Noodle Soup 74
Glass Noodle Soup with Bamboo Shoots 74
Vermicelli Soup with Tripe 75
Korean Cold Noodles 76
Korean Beef Short Ribs with Glass Noodles 77
Japanese Soba with Fish Cake and Egg 78
Chicken Soup Soba 78

Knife-Cut Noodles 80
Spicy Pork Belly Noodles 80
Cold Korean Noodles in Soy Milk 81
Spicy Sichuan Dan Dan Noodles 82
Pork and Vegetable Noodles 83
Sichuan-Style Pork and Tofu Noodles 84
Fried Chicken Soup Noodles 85
Chinese Hand-Cut Noodles 86
Preserved Mustard Greens and Pork Noodles 87
Shrimp Wonton Noodles 88
Roast Pork and Pea Shoot Noodles 89

Sweet Endings

Mango Pudding 90
Tofu Pudding Douhua 91
Cilantro and Coconut Ice Cream 92
Custard Pudding 92
Cilantro Cookies 93
Banana Coconut Fritters 93
Cantonese Steamed Sponge Cake 94
Peanut and Sesame Dumplings 94
Dragonfruit in Jasmine Tea Syrup 95
Almond Jelly 95

Foreword

Whenever I travel around Asia, I'm always overwhelmed by the abundance of noodle dishes. From the noodles themselves, which are made from wheat flour, rice flour and a lot more besides, to the cooking methods and flavors, there are so many different versions that I discover something new every time! The main theme of my travels is usually Food, so naturally I visit a variety of eating establishments when I'm going around Asia, from small local diners to food stalls and more. Each place has its own character, but I think that noodle dishes, in particular, show off the individuality of the eateries. It might be a lot of fun to just keep trying the same dish at different places to contrast and compare the similarities and differences as you travel around.

In this book, I show you how to make many of the noodle dishes that I've encountered around Asia, from those that may be familiar to you to ones you may be hearing about for the first time. Some dishes take an existing one as its inspiration, and exchange noodles for rice; there are also recipes that I've just come up with on my own, purely based on the types of noodle dishes I'd like to eat myself. I've also changed some of the ingredients from the ones used in their places of origin to ingredients that may be easier to find for a home cook. The great thing about noodle dishes is that you can have fun swapping out the ingredients, changing the cooking methods and more to come up with lots of variations. I hope that you will use this book as a starting point and add your own touches to create your very own delicious dishes.

I've also included a section at the end dedicated to Asian desserts, something that my staff strongly requested. They are my 10 favorite desserts from around Asia. I hope you'll enjoy them along with the noodle recipes.

—Maki Watanabe

How To Use This Book
- The noodle dishes chosen for this book are the ones the author believes represent the cuisines that typify Asia. The recipes of some well-known dishes may have been modified by the author to make them easier to cook.
- One tablespoon is 15 ml, and 1 teaspoon is 5 ml.
- All measurement units have been converted to the nearest practical fraction for U.S. measurements. A cup is one U.S. cup, which contains about 240 milliliters.
- When figuring out how big 1 garlic clove or 1 piece of ginger should be, use the size of the joint of your thumb as a guide. Fresh ginger root is used unpeeled for more flavor, unless otherwise noted.
- Whenever olive oil is specified, extra virgin olive oil is used.
- The heat levels specified for the stovetop and oven are meant only as a guideline. Please adjust the levels using your eyes as a guide.

Asian Noodles Used in This Book

I have used a variety of noodles from various Asian countries in this book. I have described several such as banh pho and glass or cellophane noodles throughout this book. This page describes other noodles I have used. These noodles as well as others used in this book are available at general Asian grocery stores, stores dedicated to the cuisine of a particular country, or online.

Thin Dried Thai Rice Noodles (Sen Lek) *Sen lek* means "thin noodle," and usually refers to thin dried or fresh noodles made of rice flour. These are 5/32 inches (4 mm) wide, but I've also used ones that are half that wide. You can use the thickness you prefer. There are also thick noodles called *sen yai* (see Page 25) in Thailand. You can also buy fresh *sen lek* and *sen yai* at a Thai grocery store or a well-stocked general Asian grocery store.

Chinese Egg Noodles are made with wheat flour and eggs, and come in different thicknesses. In this book I have used very thin Hong Kong-style dried egg noodles, which are sometimes labeled as chow mein noodles in North America. Egg noodles have a smooth, slippery texture.

Korean Noodles for Chilled Noodles (Naengmyeon) These chewy, springy noodles are used in many popular Korean recipes. They can be pale, made with wheat flour and other starches, or dark, containing buckwheat flour. In this book I have used both kinds. You can choose whichever type you prefer for any recipe that calls for *naengmyeon*.

Crispy Fried Chinese Noodles have been deep fried until crispy. I've used them in a couple of recipes in this book (see Pages 18-19). You can deep fry your own noodles if you prefer, but it's hard work so I usually use prefried noodles.

Fresh Chinese Noodles Most fresh Chinese noodles are made with wheat flour and an alkaline water called *kansui*. Some noodles contain eggs instead of *kansui*, while others contain both eggs and *kansui*. Chinese noodles come in various thicknesses, either straight or crinkly and so on.

Chinese Shrimp Roe Noodles are dried Chinese noodles that have shrimp roe kneaded into the dough. In this book I have used a brand that's made in Hong Kong in the Shrimp Roe Noodles (see Page 52) recipe. You can find them at Chinese grocery stores, especially if you live in an area with many expatriates from Hong Kong.

Glass or Cellophane Noodles Korean transparent glass or cellophane noodles are made with sweet potato starch. They are thicker and chewier than mung bean glass noodles from China, or potato starch or sweet potato starch glass noodles (*harusame*) from Japan. In this book I have used Korean glass noodles in Korean Stir-Fried Glass Noodles with Beef Ribs (see Page 51), a very popular Korean dish in Japan, and other types of glass noodles in several other recipes.

Dried Japanese Noodles: Udon, Hiyamugi, Handamen, Somen, Soba Since this book was originally written for a Japanese audience, it uses various dried wheat flour noodles that are easy to obtain in Japan such as udon, *handamen*, *hiyamugi* and somen. Of all these, *handamen* is the hardest to get outside Japan; the others are available at Japanese grocery stores or well-stocked general Asian groceries. Dried soba noodles, made with buckwheat and usually some wheat flour, are also available. You can use a Chinese dried wheat noodle called *mee pok* whenever *handamen* or *hiyamugi* are specified in this book. Somen (called *somyeon*) are also used in Korean cuisine.

Flavorings and Spices Used in This Book

Here are the ingredients used in this book and commonly used in Asian cooking to add flavor and spice. They are essential for creating dishes with an authentic flavor. All the ingredients can be found at general Asian grocery stores, unless noted otherwise. You may even be able to find some ingredients at your neighborhood supermarket these days.

Chinese and Taiwanese Ingredients Shaoxing wine is made with short grain or mochi rice. It's an essential ingredient in many Chinese and Taiwanese dishes. **Sesame oil** used in Chinese and other Asian cuisines is made with roasted white sesame seeds, and has a light to dark brown color. Don't use colorless sesame oil made from unroasted sesame seeds, since it won't impart the nutty flavor that is an essential part of roasted sesame oil. Both Shaoxing wine and sesame oil add richness, fragrance and depth of flavor. **Black vinegar** (see Page 8) is made with rice and/or sorghum and is aged until it has a dark brown color and a deep, malty flavor. Zhenjiang vinegar is a type of black vinegar made with rice only in Zhenjiang in Jiangsu Province.

Japanese Ingredients **Soy sauce** is widely used around Asia; in this book I have used Japanese dark or regular soy sauce, which is widely available. The base of many savory Japanese dishes is dashi, which means stock. **Rice vinegar** is the standard vinegar used in Japan; made from rice, it has a milky, slightly sweet flavor. (Don't confuse it with sushi vinegar, which may have added salt and sugar.) **Rice wine** or **sake** is made with rice, and is used to add flavor to many Japanese dishes, as well as to eliminate the gamy flavor of meat and fish. **Mirin** is a liquor that adds sweetness and richness. Sake can be used instead of Shaoxing wine in cooking.

The standard dashi is made with dried *kombu* seaweed and *katsuobushi*, salted, fermented and dried bonito that is shaved into thin flakes. (The recipes for *katsuobushi* and *kombu* dashi and for easy substitutes are on Page 9.) Another type of dashi is made with *niboshi*, small dried fish such as sardines. This type of dashi is also used in Korean cooking. You can find rice vinegar, sake, mirin, *katsuobushi* and *kombu* seaweed at Japanese grocery stores and well-stocked Korean grocery stores. *Niboshi* is available at Japanese or Korean grocery stores and well-stocked general Asian food stores.

Southeast Asian Ingredients Both Thailand and Vietnam use their own versions of fish sauce, which is made by salting and fermenting fish. The Thai version is called *nam pla*, and the Vietnamese version is called *nuoc mam*. Coconut milk is also widely used.

Ingredients That Add Heat and Spice Gochujang is a fermented paste from Korea made with rice, soybeans, barley malt, salt and red chili peppers. Although it is quite spicy, it is also sweet and savory. **Doubaniang** is a fermented spicy paste from Sichuan Province in China made with fava beans, soybeans, salt, rice and spices. It's very hot and packed with umami. **Rayu**, or *ra-yu*, is a Japanese product with Chinese roots. It's made by infusing sesame oil (sometimes another type of oil is used) with chili peppers and other ingredients. Various types of **tomato-based chili sauces** are used in Southeast Asia. Both fresh and dried chili peppers are used widely throughout Asia.

Ingredients That Add Umami or Fragrance Spices that are widely used around Asia that you may already be familiar with include cinnamon and cloves. Chinese cinnamon is different from European cinnamon, which is milder, but either can be used instead of the other. **Sichuan peppercorn** (*hua jiao*) is a spice used in Sichuan cooking that has a unique fragrance and tongue-numbing spiciness. (It shouldn't be confused with *sansho*, a similar spice used in Japanese cooking.) **Five-spice powder**, a mixture of star anise, Sichuan peppercorn, cloves, Chinese cinnamon and fennel seeds, is used throughout China and Taiwan. **Douchi** or **tochi** are fermented black soybeans that are usually chopped and added to dishes to impart a salty, umami-rich flavor. Dried foods such as **dried shiitake mushrooms** and **dried shrimp** have a lot of concentrated umami, and are used extensively around the region, especially in China.

Toppings and Condiments to Go with Noodles

The Asian way to enjoy noodles is to add lots of herbs, spices and other garnishes and condiments to make it your own. If you can't get some items at your supermarket, you can find them at general Asian grocery stores or stores dedicated to the cuisine of a particular country. It's also handy to have some popular toppings such as marinated eggs and roast pork in stock.

Fresh herbs and vegetables Try adding whole sprigs or leaves of mint, Thai basil, raw bean sprouts and Korean perilla to give an authentic Asian flavor to your noodles. For Japanese noodles, try using green shiso leaves (which differ in flavor and fragrance from Korean perilla) and *mitsuba*.

Chopped herbs and vegetables Fresh cilantro (coriander leaves) is an essential herb in Southeast Asian and Chinese cuisines. Green onions, green chili peppers and water spinach (*seri* in Japanese, *kangkong* in Chinese) are chopped to release their flavor.

Dried red chili pepper comes in powdered form, either fine or coarse, as well as in flakes and thin threads. It imparts a refined spiciness to any dish. A chili pepper mix that includes ingredients such as sesame seeds and citrus peel that's popular in Japan is *shichimi togarashi*, seven-flavor pepper.

Lemon and lime Use these citrus fruits when you want to add a refreshing taste and fragrance. Lemon has a sharp sourness, while lime is milder, with a unique scent. Citrus fruits used in Japanese cuisine as toppings and garnishes include yuzu and *kabosu*; the latter is hard to find outside Japan, so you can substitute lime.

Peanuts Peanuts are used as a topping in Thai and Vietnamese cooking in particular. It comes either roughly chopped or ground into a powder.

Chili sauce Tomato-based chili sauces are sweet as well as spicy. They are used extensively on mixed noodles, stir-fried noodles and noodle soups.

Gochujang: spicy red chili paste Korean gochujang is rich, sweet, salty and spicy. It's used as a topping for Korean Cold Noodles (Mul Naengmyeon, Page 76) or other Korean noodles where some spiciness is wanted.

Chili oil This spicy, flavorful condiment is used to add spice and flavor to Chinese and Taiwanese noodles, as well as some Japanese ones.

Black vinegar not only adds a mild sourness to dishes, it also has a rich, deep flavor. It's used as a topping for mixed, stir-fried and soup noodles. If you can't find it, a good substitute is to mix one part balsamic vinegar, one part rice wine vingar and three parts water.

How to Make Marinated Hard-Boiled Eggs

Makes 6 eggs

1 Bring a pan of water to a boil. Add 6 eggs and boil for about 7 minutes. Cool and peel.

2 Put ½ cup (100 ml) of water, ¼ cup (50 ml) each of soy sauce and mirin (or sherry) and 1 tablespoon black vinegar in a small pan and bring to a boil. Turn the heat off and put the peeled eggs in it while the sauce is still hot. Marinate for at least 2 hours.

How to Make Chinese-Style Roast Pork

Makes enough for several servings

1 Put 1 star anise, the green part of 2 leeks, 1 peeled and thinly sliced garlic clove, 1 thinly sliced piece of unpeeled ginger, ¼ cup (50 ml) each of soy sauce and mirin (or sherry) and 1 tablespoon of rice wine or sake in a bowl. Put in a 14-ounce (400 g) piece of pork shoulder, and marinate for 1 to 3 days. Reserve the marinade.

2 Heat 2 teaspoons of sesame oil in a frying pan or pan you can put in the oven. Heat over medium, and put in the drained pork. Sear the meat on all sides.

3 Add the marinade and bring to a boil. Roast in a preheated 300°F (150°C) oven for about 1 hour, turning once.

A Note on Dashi Soup Stock

Using dashi-stock powder to make instant broth is the easiest substitution. The bouillon-like powder is commonly sold in 2-oz (60-g) bags or sachets in Asian markets, specialty markets and online. Depending on the intensity and depth of flavor desired, 1 teaspoon added to boiling water typically yields from 2 to 4 cups of stock; or follow the directions on the package. Alternately, liquid concentrated dashi base is available in Asian markets and online in 13-oz (375-g) bottles, but be sure and check the sodium content first and adjust the salt content of your recipe accordingly.

If you can't find dashi-stock powder or the liquid base, then pick up a carton of prepared fish stock to impart the subtle seafood flavor your Asian noodle creations need.

How to Make Your Own Dashi Stock

Makes 4½ cups or 1 liter

1 Put a 2-inch (5-cm) square piece of dried *kombu* seaweed and 4½ cups (1 l) of cold water in a pan. Leave to soak for at least 20 to 30 minutes, overnight if you have the time. Heat over medium, and take the *kombu* seaweed out just before the water comes to a boil.

2 Add a little water to the pan, enough to lower the temperature of the water over all to about 175°F (80°C). Add ¾ cup (30 g) of *katsuobushi* or dried bonito flakes, and simmer while skimming off any foam for about 2 minutes. Turn off the heat, and leave until the *katsuobushi* has sunk to the bottom of the pan, 3 to 5 minutes.

3 Line a colander or sieve with paper towels, and place on a bowl that's a bit larger than the colander or sieve. Strain the dashi stock by pouring it through the colander or sieve.

NOTE Dashi stock can be refrigerated for 2 to 3 days, or frozen for up to a month.

PART 1

Tossed or
Mixed Noodles

This chapter contains recipes for noodles that are cooked separately, served on a plate with various other ingredients, and tossed or mixed together just before eating. It includes variations on popular items sold at food stalls in China and Taiwan, or noodles that use herbs from Thailand or Vietnam with kimchi from South Korea and more. Just have fun with the flavors and feel free to come up with your own combinations. Mix the noodles and toppings well, and enjoy the delicious and wonderful flavors!

Tossed Noodles Can be Enjoyed as a Snack or a Meal!

Fresh and dried noodles have slightly different textures and flavors.

In this book, noodles that are tossed or mixed with various ingredients are described as "tossed noodles." Besides noodles that are familiar to many readers like Zha Jiang Mian (Page 14) and Bibimbap (Page 28), I hope you will try noodles from different cuisines such as Rat Na from Thailand (Page 25) or Bun Cha from Vietnam (Page 27).

In fact, out of all the noodle types in the wide and deep world of Asian noodles, tossed noodles are my favorites, and I make and eat them all the time at home as well as during my travels. My special favorite is a simple tossed noodle dish from Taiwan where black vinegar, a sweet soy sauce, deep fried shallots and leeks are tossed with freshly boiled noodles. It's so easy to make and hits the spot so perfectly; plus I love that it can be enjoyed as a casual snack rather than a full-on meal. I've been taking a trip to Taiwan every year over the past decade, and every time I have this simple dish several times, enjoying the differences and variations at this or that eatery.

Add Toppings and Flavors to Suit Your Tastes
Tossed noodles aren't just limited to Taiwan, they exist in Vietnam, Thailand and other countries in Southeast Asia too. What they all have in common is that the noodles come with a ton of toppings, and various condiments are

HOW TO BOIL FRESH CHINESE NOODLES

1 Bring plenty of water to a boil (a rule of thumb is to use 1 liter or 4 cups per serving of dried Chinese noodles). Once it's boiling, add the noodles.

2 When the noodles start to loosen up, give them a stir to loosen them even more, and cook them for the amount of time specified on the packet.

3 Drain the noodles as soon as they're cooked, and shake off all the moisture completely.

Tongs are handy for mixing the noodles and the other ingredients.

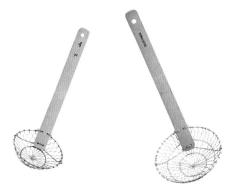

There are many different types of noodle strainers, from the shapes to the materials they're made from. Choosing between them is fun!

available at the table that people can add to customize their noodles to their hearts' content. Whether it's adding chopped-up cilantro (coriander leaves) or other herbs, scattering on some peanuts, squeezing on lemon or lime juice, or adding hot spices or vinegar, it's each according to their own tastes and how they're feeling that day! Even if everyone orders the same item from the menu, the tastes on each person's plate can be different, and become more and more complicated or even change flavors entirely as they eat. That's the fun thing about tossed noodles. I encourage you to add your own toppings and flavors, too, to come up with your own unique tossed-noodle versions.

The Key to Boiling Noodles Is to Drain Off the Water Properly

For the Chinese and Taiwanese tossed noodles in this chapter, I've used fresh Chinese noodles. They're made primarily with wheat flour and an alkaline water called *kansui,* but there are also noodles made with eggs, as well as ones that don't use *kansui.* Try choosing the ones you like, depending on the dish. With all noodles that are boiled, the key is to drain off the cooking water very well. In addition, if you are using Chinese noodles in chilled dishes like *hiyashi chuka,* for the best taste, drain the noodles into a colander as soon as they're boiled, and then firm them up by rinsing them under cold running water.

HOW TO BOIL DRIED CHINESE NOODLES

1 Bring plenty of water to a boil (a rule of thumb is to use 1 liter or 4 cups per serving of dried Chinese noodles). Once it's boiling, add the noodles.

2 When the noodles start to loosen up, give them a stir to loosen them even more, and cook them for the amount of time specified on the packet.

3 Drain the noodles as soon as they're cooked, and shake off all the moisture completely.

Beijing-Style Pork Noodles with Black Bean Sauce Zha Jiang Mian

The salty-sweet sauce mixed with the cubed pork and crunchy bamboo matches well with the wide Chinese noodles. It's a very filling dish too.

Serves 2

7 oz (200 g) pork shoulder, cubed

1 cup (120 g) cooked bamboo shoots (canned or vacuum-packed), diced

½ onion

2 teaspoons sesame oil

1-inch piece of ginger, peeled and finely chopped

8 oz (250 g) fresh flat Chinese egg noodles

5 sprigs cilantro (coriander leaves), roughly chopped

2 teaspoons toasted white sesame seeds

Sauce

2 tablespoons *tian mian jiang* (fermented salty-sweet black bean sauce)

2 tablespoons Shaoxing wine or pale dry sherry

1 tablespoon soy sauce

½ teaspoon salt

1 Cut the pork, bamboo shoots and onion into ⅓-inch (1-cm) dice.

2 Heat a frying pan over medium, and add the sesame oil and ginger. When you can smell the oil, add the pork, bamboo shoots and onion, and stir fry until the pork turns white.

3 Mix the Sauce ingredients together and add to the frying pan. Stir fry until the Sauce is thick and no longer watery.

4 Cook the noodles following the instructions on the packet. (If there are no instructions, bring a generous amount of water to a boil in a large pan. Add the noodles, and cook for 3 to 5 minutes, testing for doneness.) Drain off the water, and arrange on serving plates. Add the stir-fried mixture. Top with the cilantro and sesame seeds.

....

NOTE This is a Chinese noodle dish that's popular everywhere. Here I have used pork shoulder cut into dice, instead of the usual minced pork. Because the ingredients are quite substantial, I combined them with wide noodles. If you add some whole fermented black soybeans (called *douchi* or *tochi*), the dish will be even more authentic.

Sichuan Steamed Chicken Noodles

The juicy steamed chicken is mouthwateringly delicious! If you want this to be spicy, try adding more hot sesame chili oil (*rayu*).

Serves 2

2 large boneless chicken thighs, skin on, about 10 oz (300 g) total

2 green onions, green part only

1 garlic clove, peeled and thinly sliced

1-inch piece of unpeeled ginger, thinly sliced

3 tablespoons Shaoxing wine or sake

½ teaspoon salt

2 tablespoons sesame oil

3 tablespoons soy sauce

2 tablespoons black vinegar

8 oz (240 g) fresh Chinese lo mein noodles

5 sprigs fresh cilantro (coriander leaves), roughly chopped

1 tablespoon hot sesame chili oil

1 Slice into the thickest part of the chicken thigh sideways (parallel to your cutting board) part of the way, then fold the meat out so it's a uniform thickness overall. (Alternatively, pound the meat gently with the side of your knife or a meat tenderizer until it's of uniform thickness.) Line the bottom of a bamboo steamer basket (or a heatproof plate) with parchment paper, and place the chicken on it. Put the green onion, garlic and ginger on top, and sprinkle with the Shaoxing wine, salt and sesame oil. (If using a plate, put the plate in the steamer basket.) Bring a pot of water to a boil, place the steamer basket on top, and steam the chicken for about 8 minutes.

2 Mix 1 tablespoon of the water used to steam the chicken with the soy sauce and vinegar.

3 Cook the fresh Chinese noodles following the instructions on the packet. (If there are no instructions, bring a generous amount of water to a boil in a large pan. Add the noodles, and cook for 2 to 3 minutes, testing for doneness.) Drain off the cooking water, and arrange the noodles on serving plates. Slice the chicken into bite-sized pieces and put on top of the noodles. Top with the chopped cilantro, and sprinkle on the sauce from Step 2 and hot sesame chili oil.

NOTE The original name for the chicken in this Sichuan dish, *kou shui ji*, means "saliva chicken." Apparently it got this name because it's mouthwateringly delicious. Use thigh meat with its skin on, steamed with lots of aromatics, cooked until it's silky and tender. I use a sauce with fragrant black vinegar, soy and the chicken's own juices.

Sliced Pork and Green Onion Noodles

Tender pieces of pork coated with a spicy sauce go well with thin egg noodles and crunchy green onions. I just can't get enough of this simple dish.

Serves 2

2 tablespoons rice wine or sake
12 thin slices pork belly (about 7 oz or 200 g)
1 teaspoon coarsely ground red chili pepper
1 tablespoon black vinegar
2 tablespoons soy sauce
1½ tablespoons sesame oil
8 oz (250 g) fresh Chinese thin lo mein egg noodles
4 green onions, thinly sliced

1 Add the sake to a pot of boiling water. Lower the heat to a simmer and add the pork. Cook until the pork just changes color and turns white, then drain. Pat the pork dry with paper towels, and put into a bowl.

2 Combine the ground red chili pepper, black vinegar, soy sauce and sesame oil in a separate bowl. Add half of this mixture to the bowl with the pork and mix to combine.

3 Cook the fresh Chinese noodles following the instructions on the packet. (If there are no instructions, bring a generous amount of water to a boil in a large pan. Add the noodles, and cook for about 2 minutes, testing for doneness.) Drain off the cooking water, and arrange the noodles on serving plates. Top with the pork, chopped green onions and the remaining sauce.

....

NOTE Roast pork is often used for dishes like this, but what I do when I want to eat quickly is to use presliced pork belly that's sold at Asian grocery stores, as in this easy recipe. The pork only takes a few minutes to cook, then you mix it with the sauce and green onions and enjoy.

Pork and Black Vinegar Chilled Noodles Hiyashi Chuka

The ripped-up green shiso (Japanese perilla) leaves have a lovely fresh flavor in this refined chilled noodle dish. It's a great dish to add to your repertoire of summertime cold noodles.

Serves 2

7 oz (200 g) boiled pork (see below)
1 small Japanese cucumber, or ½ a large
    cucumber, deseeded
8 oz (250 g) fresh Chinese lo mein
    noodles
5 green shiso leaves, or mint or Thai basil
1-inch piece of ginger, peeled and grated
½ teaspoon sugar
2 tablespoons black vinegar
1 tablespoon sesame oil
2 teaspoons toasted white sesame seeds
Chinese or Japanese hot mustard,
    to serve

1 Slice the boiled pork ⅓ inch (1 cm) thick. Cut the cucumber into very thin strips.
2 Cook the fresh Chinese noodles following the instructions on the packet. (If there are no instructions, bring a generous amount of water to a boil in a large pan. Add the noodles, and cook for 2 to 3 minutes, testing for doneness.) Drain, then run under cold water in a bowl, changing the water frequently until the noodles are completely cooled. Drain well, and arrange the noodles on serving plates.
3 Top the noodles with the sliced pork. Tear the shiso leaves into bite-sized pieces and scatter them on top. Mix the grated ginger, sugar, black vinegar and sesame oil together, and pour over the noodles. Sprinkle with the sesame seeds, and serve the mustard on the side.

. . . .

NOTE When summer comes around, I always get an urge to eat chilled noodles. In Japan, this type of chilled noodle dish is called *hiyashi chuka*, which means "chilled Chinese," but it's actually a Japanese rather than a Chinese dish. You can vary the toppings and sauce in many ways, but here I've kept it refreshing and simple by using green shiso leaves and cucumber with a vinegar-based sauce.

Boiled pork is very useful to have on hand. Drain well before storing in the refrigerator or freezer.

Canton-Style Crispy Shrimp and Pork Noodles

These crispy noodles, especially when they are freshly fried, as well as the ones that have been drenched in the seafood-rich sauce, are both very tasty!

Serves 2

5 oz (150 g) thinly sliced pork

2 tablespoons cornstarch

1 small leek, white part only

3 fresh wood ear or shiitake mushrooms (or 3 dried wood ear or shiitake, soaked in warm water until softened)

2 teaspoons plus 1 tablespoon sesame oil

1-inch piece of ginger, peeled and finely shredded

6 to 8 peeled and deveined medium shrimp, about 3 oz (90 g)

6 boiled peeled quail eggs (sold in cans or vacuum packs) or 2 boiled chicken eggs, cut in quarters

2 tablespoons rice wine or sake

1¼ cups (300ml) water

1 tablespoon soy sauce

½ teaspoon salt

6 oz (175 g) ready-to-eat fried crispy noodles (see the note for alternative)

1 Slice the pork into thin strips, and dust with the potato starch or cornstarch. Cut the leek into thin slices diagonally. Remove the stems from the wood ear mushrooms and cut into bite-sized pieces.

2 Heat a frying pan over medium heat, and add 1 tablespoon of sesame oil and ginger. When the oil is fragrant add the pork, leek and mushrooms, and stir fry until the leek is turning limp.

3 Add the shrimp, quail eggs, sake, water and soy sauce to the pan. Bring to a boil while skimming off any foam. Turn the heat down to low, and simmer for about 6 minutes. Add the soy sauce, salt and 2 teaspoons of sesame oil. Simmer until the sauce has thickened and is creamy.

4 Put the crispy noodles on plates, and top with the mixture from Step 3.

NOTE The Cantonese style of cooking blends a variety of ingredients together and flavors them simply. Here I have taken advantage of the natural umami in ingredients like pork, shrimp and mushrooms.

If you can't find ready-to-eat crispy noodles, heat vegetable oil to 350°F (180°C) in a wok or large saucepan. Fry 7 oz (240 g) of fresh chow mein noodles in two batches until lightly browned and crisp, about 2 minutes. Drain off the oil. Alternatively, you can pan fry the chow mein noodles in two batches in a frying pan with a generous amount of oil, turning occasionally, until browned and crispy on both sides.

Crab Omelette Crispy Noodles

Adding broccoli to a crab omelette (*kanikama*) gives it a fresh twist. The thick, creamy sauce goes really well with this too.

Serves 2

½ cup (100 g) diced broccoli

1 small leek, white part only

4 eggs

¼ cup (110 g) cooked crabmeat, canned or fresh

1-inch piece of ginger, peeled and finely chopped

1 tablespoon rice wine or sake

2 tablespoons soy sauce, divided

2 tablespoons plus 1 teaspoon sesame oil, divided

1 tablespoon black vinegar

Pinch of salt

2 teaspoons cornstarch

3 tablespoons water

6 oz (175 g) ready-to-eat fried crispy noodles (see the note on the previous page for alternative)

Chili pepper flakes, to taste

1 Cut the broccoli into small pieces. Finely slice the leek.

2 Break the eggs into a bowl. Drain the crabmeat, reserving 2 tablespoons of the liquid. Add the crabmeat, the reserved liquid, the chopped ginger, sake and 1 tablespoon of soy sauce to the bowl, and mix well to combine.

3 Heat up 1 tablespoon of sesame oil in a frying pan over medium and add half of the egg-and-crab mixture. Stir gently until the eggs are soft set. Turn the heat down to low, and cook the omelette for about 5 minutes. Flip over and cook the other side for another 5 minutes. Repeat with the other half of the egg-and-crab mixture.

4 Put 1 tablespoon of soy sauce, the black vinegar, salt, cornstarch and water in a small pan, and mix well to combine. Cook over medium heat while stirring until the sauce is thickened. When the sauce comes to a boil, add 1 teaspoon of sesame oil and mix well.

5 Arrange the crispy noodles on serving plates. Put the omelettes on top and pour the sauce over. Sprinkle on some chili pepper flakes to taste.

....

NOTE I have added broccoli to a classic Cantonese recipe, egg foo young with crab. The combination of textures when it's served on crispy noodles makes this a fun dish.

Five-Spice Pork Noodles

Mix the five-spice-scented pork, soft-poached egg, green onions and nori seaweed with the noodles so the flavors are evenly distributed. Then try to resist having seconds.

Serves 2

2 teaspoons sesame oil

1 garlic clove, peeled and finely chopped

1-inch piece of ginger, peeled and finely chopped

7 oz (200 g) ground pork

½ teaspoon five-spice powder

1 tablespoon soy sauce

1 tablespoon rice wine or sake

1 tablespoon black vinegar

4 green onions

1 sheet roasted nori seaweed

7 oz (200 g) thick dried udon noodles, or similar thick wheat flour noodles

2 soft-boiled eggs (see instructions)

1 Heat up a frying pan over medium heat. Add the sesame oil, garlic and ginger. When the oil is fragrant, add the pork, and stir fry until the pork turns white. Add the five-spice powder, soy sauce, sake and black vinegar, and continue stir frying until there is little moisture left in the pan.

2 Chop the green onions, and rip up the nori seaweed into bite-sized pieces.

3 Cook the noodles following the instructions on the packet. Drain well and arrange in serving bowls. Top with the pork mixture, green onions, nori and eggs. Mix well before eating.

Soft-boiled eggs: The eggs used in this recipe are boiled until the white is barely set. Only use very fresh or pasteurized eggs, or cook the eggs a little longer for safety reasons. Bring to a boil enough water to cover the eggs in a pan. Turn off the heat, and add the eggs in their shells carefully, using a ladle. Cover the pan and leave the eggs to cook in the residual heat for 10 to 12 minutes for very soft-set eggs, or longer for a firmer set. Break the eggs over the noodles if very soft set, or peel, halve and put on top.

....

NOTE This is a type of noodle dish that can be found at food stalls anywhere in Taiwan, but it's very popular in Japan too. I have used thick udon noodles for this version, which I never get tired of eating.

Taiwanese Chicken Noodles Ji Rou Mian

I recommend making this simple quick dish as a snack when you're feeling a bit peckish. It always hits the spot!

Serves 2

1 large boneless chicken breast, skin on, about 7 oz (200 g)
1 tablespoon Shaoxing wine or sake
1 tablespoon soy sauce
1 tablespoon sesame oil
1 tablespoon fish sauce
1 tablespoon black vinegar
1 small leek, white part only
4 sprigs fresh cilantro (coriander leaves)
7 oz (200 g) *mee pok* or similar thin dried wheat noodles
Toasted white sesame seeds, to garnish

1 Slice into the thickest part of the chicken thigh sideways (parallel to your cutting board) part of the way, then fold the meat out so it's a uniform thickness overall. (Alternatively, pound the meat gently with the side of your knife or a meat tenderizer until it's of uniform thickness.) Place the chicken on a heatproof plate. Combine the Shaoxing wine or sake, soy sauce and sesame oil, and sprinkle onto the chicken. Bring a pot of water to a boil. Put the plate with the chicken in a steamer basket and put the steamer on top of the pot of boiling water. Steam over high heat for about 7 minutes. Leave until cool enough to handle, remove the skin and cut the chicken into bite-sized pieces.
2 Combine the fish sauce and black vinegar with 4 to 5 tablespoons of the chicken steaming water.
3 Make several lengthwise cuts down the leek. Remove the core, slice into thin shreds, then chop finely. Put the cut-up leek in a bowl of water for a couple of minutes, then drain. Chop the cilantro roughly.
4 Cook the noodles following the instructions on the package. Drain well. Arrange the noodles in bowls, top with the chicken, sauce, leek and cilantro, and sprinkle on some sesame seeds.

....

NOTE This recipe is based on one of my favorite dishes, Taiwanese chicken and rice (*jirou fan*), where rice is topped with steamed chicken and sauce, and mixed together before eating. Here I have paired the chicken and sauce with noodles instead of rice.

Simple Sesame and Green Onion Noodles

This is an ultrasimple noodle dish that you can slurp up as a snack. When the toppings are mixed in, your senses are filled with the wonderful fragrance of sesame.

Serves 2

4 thin green onions
1 small leek, white part only
10 oz (300 g) fresh *mee pok* or 7 oz (200 g) dried thin wheat noodles
4 tablespoons ground sesame paste or tahini
1½ tablespoons black vinegar
2 tablespoons soy sauce
Pinch of salt
1 tablespoon hot sesame chili oil

1 Chop the green onions and leek finely. Soak the leek in cold water for 5 minutes, and drain.
2 Cook the noodles following the instructions on the packet. Drain well, and put into 2 serving bowls. Top with the chopped green onion and leek. Combine the sesame paste, black vinegar, soy sauce and salt. Pour the mixture and the hot sesame chili oil over the noodles, and mix well before eating.

Dried Shrimp and Black Bean Sauce Noodles

The stir-fried topping with lots of umami-rich ingredients really completes the dish! Mix everything together well, and enjoy the refreshing flavors of the lemon and celery.

Serves 2

¼ cup (50 g) dried shrimp
1 tablespoon fermented black beans (*douchi*)
1 small leek, white part only
½ celery stalk
1 tablespoon sesame oil
1-inch piece of ginger, peeled and finely chopped
2 tablespoons rice wine or sake
1 tablespoon black vinegar
1 tablespoon soy sauce
¼ teaspoon salt
8 oz (250 g) fresh Chinese lo mein noodles
1 cup (50 g) radish sprouts or bean sprouts
2 lemon wedges

1 Soak the dried shrimp in enough lukewarm water to cover for about 30 minutes until softened. Drain and chop roughly, reserving the soaking liquid. Chop the fermented black soybeans roughly. Chop the leek finely.
2 Remove the tough outer strings from the celery stalk. Chop the stalk and the leaves finely.
3 Heat a frying pan over medium. Add 1 teaspoon of the sesame oil and the chopped ginger. When the oil is fragrant, add the shrimp, fermented black soybeans and leek to the pan, and stir fry briefly.
4 Add the sake, black vinegar, soy sauce and salt to the frying pan with the soaking liquid from the shrimp. Simmer while stirring until there is very little moisture left in the pan.
5 Cook the noodles following the instructions on the packet. (If there are no instructions, bring a generous amount of water to a boil in a large pan. Add the noodles, and cook for 3 to 5 minutes, testing for doneness.) Drain off the water, and arrange in serving bowls. Cut the roots off the radish sprouts. Put the chopped celery, stir-fried shrimp mixture and radish sprouts on the noodles. Serve with lemon wedges.

NOTE Lurofan, a dish consisting of simmered pork poured over rice, is a much-loved everyday standard in Taiwan. Here I have combined the simmered pork with noodles, and thickened the sauce so that it coats the noodles well.

A Be sure to cut the protein into uniform cubes, so all the pieces will cook evenly.

B Make sure the cornstarch is throughly dissolved in the water before adding it to the pan.

Braised Soy Pork Noodles

This dish is usually made with rice, but by changing the rice to noodles it takes on a fresh new character. The soft-boiled egg topping is a must.

Serves 2

7 oz (200 g) pork belly

3 teaspoons sesame oil

1-inch piece of ginger, peeled and finely chopped

1 star anise

1 tablespoon oyster sauce

3½ tablespoons Shaoxing wine or pale dry sherry

1½ tablespoons soy sauce

2 teaspoons cornstarch

⅓ cup (80 ml) water

2 baby bok choi

1 soft-boiled egg, peeled

10 oz (300 g) fresh *mee pok* or 7 oz (200 g) similar dried medium-thin wheat noodles

1 Cut the pork belly into ⅓-inch (1-cm) cubes **(see photo A)**.

2 Heat up a frying pan over medium. Add 1 teaspoon of the sesame oil and the chopped ginger. When the oil is fragrant, add the cubed pork, and stir fry until the meat changes color and turns white.

3 Add the star anise, oyster sauce, Shaoxing wine, soy sauce and water to the frying pan. Bring to a boil, then turn the heat down to low and simmer for about 12 minutes. Dissolve the cornstarch in 1 tablespoon of water, and add to the frying pan while stirring to thicken the sauce **(see photo B)**. Add the remaining 2 teaspoons of sesame oil and stir.

4 Cook the bok choi in boiling water for about 30 seconds, drain well and cut in half lengthwise. Cut the soft-boiled egg in half.

5 Cook the noodles following the instructions on the packet. Drain well. Arrange the noodles in serving bowls, and top with the pork and bok choi.

Dry Tom Yum Noodles

The Thai use the word *haeng*, meaning "dry," to describe this dish, a *tom yum* noodle dish without soup. The paste is stir fried with ground pork and mixed in with the noodles.

Serves 2

1 tablespoon sesame oil
7 oz (200 g) ground pork
2 teaspoons *tom yum* paste (see below)
2 tablespoons rice wine or sake
1½ tablespoons fish sauce
7 oz (200 g) dried Chinese wheat noodles
½ cup (120 g) soybean sprouts
2 sprigs fresh Thai basil leaves
2 tablespoons roughly chopped peanuts
½ lime, cut into wedges

1 Heat the oil over medium. Add the ground pork and *tom yum* paste. When the meat changes color, add the sake and the fish sauce, and continue stir frying until there is little moisture left.
2 Cook the noodles following the instructions on the packet, and drain well. Arrange the cooked noodles on serving plates, and top with the meat and sauce. Scatter with the sprouts, basil and peanuts and squeeze with lime juice.

NOTE You can buy prepared *tom yum* paste in Asian grocery stores. To make it, grind 1 green chili, a 6-inch (15-cm) piece of lemongrass, 1 garlic clove and one kaffir lime leaf in a mortar.

Beef & Coriander Glass Noodles

Lemongrass gives these noodles a refreshing aftertaste. You can enjoy this Thai dish like a salad, or as a side dish to go with rice.

Serves 2

½ red onion
2 tablespoons rice wine or sake
4 oz (120 g) thinly sliced beef ribeye or sirloin
1 green chili pepper, cut in half lengthwise
2 stalks lemongrass, crushed
1-inch piece of fresh ginger, peeled and minced
2 tablespoons lemon juice
2 tablespoons fish sauce
6 oz (175 g) dried glass or cellophane noodles
5 sprigs fresh cilantro (coriander leaves), roughly chopped
2 tablespoons sesame oil

1 Slice the onion thinly lengthwise. Put the slices in a bowl of cold water and soak for 3 minutes. Drain well.
2 Bring a pan of water to a boil and add the sake. Separate the beef into single slices, and put one slice at a time into the boiling water. Take the beef out as soon as it changes color, and drain on paper towels.
3 Combine the onion, beef, chili pepper, lemongrass, ginger, lemon juice and fish sauce in a bowl and mix.
4 Bring another pot of water to a boil. Add the glass noodles, cook for 2 minutes and drain. Add the noodles to the mixture from Step 3, and mix well to coat them in the flavors. Add the chopped cilantro/coriander and sesame oil, and mix.

NOTE Wide (about ⅓ inch or 1 cm) dried noodles made of rice and tapioca flour called *sen yai* are used for this dish. Fresh noodles can be used instead. Both are available at Asian grocery stores. Thin noodles are called *sen lek*.

A Sometimes your hands are your best tools. Make sure the pieces are evenly coated with the cornstarch.

B Don't overcook the greens, as they'll be getting additional heat while the eggs set.

Thai Rice Noodles with Pork and Spinach Rat Na

This hearty, rich stew is a great accompaniment to plain rice or rice noodles. The creamy broth coats the thick rice noodles for a perfect bite every time.

Serves 2

5 oz (150 g) thinly sliced pork shoulder

2 teaspoons cornstarch

1 bunch water spinach *(kangkong)* or watercress

4 teaspoons sesame oil

1 kaffir lime leaf (optional)

3½ tablespoons rice wine or sake

2 tablespoons fish sauce

⅔ cup (150 ml) water

2 eggs, beaten

1-inch piece of fresh ginger, peeled and grated

6 oz (175 g) dried wide rice noodles

1 Cut up the pork into bite-sized pieces, and coat with the cornstarch *(see photo A)*.

2 Chop up the water spinach or watercress roughly.

3 Heat up 2 teaspoons of the sesame oil in a frying pan over medium, add the cut-up pork and kaffir lime leaf, and stir fry until the meat changes color and turns white.

4 Add the sake, fish sauce and water to the pan. Bring to a boil while skimming off any residue. Add the water spinach and simmer while stirring until it turns limp. Add the beaten eggs and grated ginger *(see photo B)*. When the eggs are soft-set and creamy, stir in the remaining sesame oil.

5 Cook the noodles following the directions on the package. Drain well, arrange in serving bowls and pour the pork mixture over it.

Squid and Lemongrass Noodles with Peanut Sauce

I've added lemongrass to peanut sauce, a Vietnamese staple, for a refreshing twist. Mix the sauce and other ingredients well before eating.

Serves 2

2 small fresh squid, about 4 oz (120 g) total
2 tablespoons rice wine or sake
2 stalks lemongrass
6 oz (175 g) dried medium-width rice noodles
6 springs fresh cilantro (coriander leaves), roughly chopped
½ red Thai chili pepper, deseeded and chopped

Sauce

4 tablespoons peanut butter
2 tablespoons lemon juice
2 tablespoons fish sauce

1 Remove the innards, transparent "quill" and skin from the squid. Slice into ⅓ inch (1 cm) wide pieces. Bring enough water to cover the squid to a boil in a pan and add the sake and 1 lemongrass stalk. Add the squid and boil for 2 minutes. Take off the heat and leave to cool. Drain the squid.
2 Finely chop the remaining lemongrass stalk. Add to the Sauce ingredients and mix.
3 Cook the rice noodles following the instructions on the packet. Drain, then rinse under cold running water to firm up the texture. Drain well, and put into serving bowls. Top with the squid, Sauce, cilantro and chili pepper.

Vietnamese River Noodles with Pork and Shrimp Mi Quang

This noodle dish comes from Da Nang, a city in central Vietnam. There are various kinds of toppings, but here I have used pork, shrimp and lots of herbs.

Serves 2

4 oz (120 g) pork belly
1 tablespoon sesame oil
1 garlic clove, peeled and thinly sliced
4 large shrimp, about 2 oz (50 g) total
2 tablespoons rice wine or sake
6 oz (175 g) dried flat rice noodles
⅓ cup (10 g) fresh mint leaves
1 bunch watercress, chopped
3 green onions, cut into 2-inch (5-cm) pieces
1 tablespoon ground peanuts

Sauce

1 teaspoon sugar
2 tablespoons lemon juice
2 tablespoons fish sauce

1 Cut the pork into ⅓ inch (1 cm) cubes. Heat up the sesame oil and garlic in a skillet over medium. When the oil is fragrant, add the pork cubes. Stir fry while wiping out the excess fat in the pan frequently with paper towels until the pork cubes are brown and crisp.
2 Devein the shrimp. Put the rice wine/sake in a pan with water enough to cover the shrimp and bring to a boil. Add the shrimp and boil for 2 minutes. Turn the heat off and leave the shrimp to cool in the cooking water. Once cool, take the shrimp out and drain.
3 Cook the rice noodles following the instructions on the packet. Drain, then rinse under cold running water to firm up the texture. Drain well, and put into serving bowls.
4 Top the noodles with the pork, shrimp, mint leaves, watercress and green onions. Combine the Sauce ingredients and pour over the noodles. Sprinkle with the ground peanuts.

NOTE Although they may not be as familiar as pho, *bun* or thin rice noodles are also a staple noodle in Vietnam. This dish of *bun* topped with sweet-and-sour shredded vegetables, herbs and meatballs is a typical Vietnamese noodle dish. It's also delicious with deep-fried spring rolls (*nems*) instead of the meatballs.

A Adding mint leaves to meatballs gives them a Southeast Asian flavor.

B Once you form the meatballs, shallow fry them in a small amount of oil. Turn them to brown them on all sides.

Vietnamese Rice Noodles with Meatballs Bun Cha

With minted meatballs as well as sweet-and-sour shredded vegetables, this noodle dish is packed with the flavors of Vietnam.

Serves 2

Olive oil, for frying
4-inch (10-cm) piece of daikon radish
⅓ carrot
½ teaspoon salt
5 oz (150 g) dried thin rice noodles
Few sprigs of mixed fresh herbs, such as mint, Thai basil and cilantro, to garnish

Meatball Mixture

7 oz (200 g) ground pork
½ onion, peeled and minced
4 fresh mint leaves, chopped
1 garlic clove, peeled and minced
1-inch piece ginger, peeled and minced
½ egg, beaten
1 tablespoon cornstarch
1 tablespoon rice wine or sake
⅓ teaspoon salt

Sauce

½ red Thai chili or serrano pepper, deseeded and minced
1 teaspoon sugar
2 tablespoons black vinegar
1 tablespoon lime juice
1½ tablespoons fish sauce

1 Put the Meatball Mixture ingredients in a bowl and mix well. *(see photo A)* Form into 1⅓ to 1½ inch (3 to 4 cm) diameter meatballs.

2 Heat up about ½ inch (1½ cm) of olive oil in a pan. Add the meatballs, and shallow fry until half cooked through for about 7 minutes, turning occasionally. Drain off the oil. *(see photo B)*

3 Shred the daikon radish and carrot very finely. Sprinkle with salt and rub it in well. When the vegetables are limp, squeeze them tightly to eliminate any extra moisture. Combine the Sauce ingredients in a bowl and mix well. Add 2 tablespoons of the Sauce to the shredded vegetables in another bowl and mix to coat.

4 Cook the rice noodles following the instructions on the packet. Drain, and rinse under cold running water to firm up the texture. Drain well and arrange in serving bowls. Top with the meatballs, shredded vegetables and herbs. Pour on the rest of the Sauce.

Spicy Cold Korean Buckwheat Noodles

Bibimbap is a spicy chilled Korean-style noodle dish where a gochujang-based sauce is mixed with the noodles. The spiciness is tempered with the refreshing sweetness of the tomatoes.

Serves 2

6 slices boiled pork, about 4 oz (120 g) total
¼ cup (60 g) chopped cabbage kimchi
8 oz (250 g) Korean dried buckwheat or sweet potato noodles
4 small or 8 cherry tomatoes
½ cup (20 g) radish sprouts, trimmed
2 teaspoons toasted white sesame seeds, to garnish

Sauce

1 teaspoon gochujang (Korean red chili paste)
½ clove garlic, peeled and minced
1-inch piece of ginger, peeled and grated
2 tablespoons black vinegar
2 tablespoons soy sauce
2 tablespoons sesame oil

1 Slice the pork into ⅓ inch (1 cm) wide slices. Chop up the kimchi.
2 Cook the noodles following the instructions on the packet. Rinse with plenty of cold running water until completely cooled and firm. Drain well and put into a bowl. Combine the Sauce ingredients, mix with the noodles until the Sauce coats the noodles well, and distribute the noodles in serving bowls.
3 Put the sliced pork, chopped tomatoes and sprouts on top of the noodles. Sprinkle with the sesame seeds.

Korean Raw Fish and Perilla Buckwheat Noodles

I've turned *hoe*, a classic Korean dish made with raw fish filets like sashimi, into a noodle dish. I've used buckwheat *naengmyeon* here, but you can use sweet potato noodles if you prefer.

Serves 2

6 oz (175 g) sashimi-grade whitefish filets such as sea bream
1 small leek, white part only
8 oz (250 g) Korean dried buckwheat or sweet potato noodles
5 perilla leaves (or mint or Thai basil) torn in pieces
Freshly ground dried chili pepper, to taste

Sauce

½ clove garlic, peeled and minced
1-inch piece of ginger, peeled and grated
2 tablespoons black vinegar
2 tablespoons soy sauce
2 tablespoons sesame oil

1 Slice the fish into ⅓ inch (7-8 mm) thick slices.
2 Make several slits in the leek. Remove the core, and shred finely. Put into a bowl of cold water for a few minutes, then drain well.
3 Cook the noodles following the instructions on the packet. Rinse with plenty of cold running water until completely cooled and firm.
4 Drain well and put into a bowl. Combine the Sauce ingredients. Combine ½ of the Sauce with the noodles and mix until the Sauce coats the noodles well, and distribute the noodles on serving plates. Arrange the fish slices on top.
5 Top the noodles with the perilla leaves and the shredded leek or green onion. Pour the rest of the Sauce over the noodles, and sprinkle with ground chili pepper to taste.

How to Cook Japanese Noodles

Here I show you how to cook fresh soba noodles, dried somen noodles and frozen udon noodles, three very popular types of noodles in Japan. If you know the little things to pay attention to, your noodle dishes will turn out so much better.

HOW TO COOK FRESH SOBA NOODLES

1 Bring a generous amount of water (the rule of thumb is 4½ cups or 1 liter per hank of fresh soba noodles) to a boil. Once the water is boiling, add the soba noodles while loosening them up with your hands.
2 When the water comes back to a rolling boil, add about half a cup of water to calm down the boil a little.
3 Stir the noodles using tongs or cooking chopsticks. Cook the noodles for the length of time indicated on the packet. Adjust the heat, so that the pot doesn't boil over.
4 Drain the noodles as soon as they are cooked. Rinse and gently rub the noodles under cold running water until there is no stickiness on the surface and the texture is firm. Drain very well.
5 If you're making a cold noodle dish, use the noodles as is. If you're making a warm noodle dish, heat the noodles up briefly by passing them through freshly boiled water.

HOW TO COOK DRIED SOMEN NOODLES

HOW TO COOK FROZEN UDON NOODLES

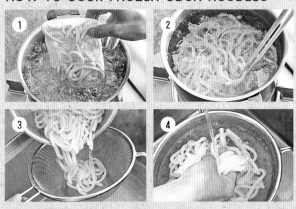

1 Bring a generous amount of water (the rule of thumb is 4½ cups, or 1 liter, per 3½ ounces, or 100 grams) of dried somen noodles to a boil. Once the water is boiling, scatter in the somen noodles.
2 Stir the noodles using tongs or cooking chopsticks. Cook the noodles for the length of time indicated on the packet (usually from 90 seconds to 2 minutes). Adjust the heat so that the pot doesn't boil over.
3 Drain the noodles as soon as they are cooked. Rinse and gently rub the noodles under cold running water until there is no stickiness on the surface and the texture is firm.
4 Drain the noodles very well.

1 Bring a generous amount of water (the rule of thumb is 4½ cups or 1 liter per hank or packet of frozen udon noodles) to a boil. When the water is at a full boil, add the frozen noodles.
2 When the water comes back to a rolling boil, cook the noodles for the length of time indicated on the packet while stirring them with long cooking chopsticks (usually 2 to 3 minutes).
3 Drain the noodles as soon as they are cooked. If you're making a warm noodle dish, you can use them at this point.
4 If you're making a cold noodle dish, rinse and gently rub the noodles under cold running water until they are completely cooled and have a firm texture. Drain well.

**Somen Noodles with Eggplant and
Grated Daikon**

Somen with Walnut Sauce

Somen Noodles with Eggplant and Grated Daikon

Let the sauce sink into the soft deep-fried eggplant, then mix well with the somen (thin Japanese wheat noodles) and the grated daikon radish.

Serves 2

1¼ cups (300 ml) dashi stock **(see Page 9)**
2 tablespoons rice wine or sake
1½ tablespoons soy sauce
¼ teaspoon of salt
2 to 3 small Japanese eggplants, about 8 oz (225 g) total
Vegetable oil, for frying
4-inch (10-cm) piece of daikon radish
6 oz (175 g) dried somen noodles

1 Put the dashi stock, rice wine/sake, soy sauce and salt in a small pan and bring to a boil over medium heat. Take off the heat and leave to cool to room temperature. Chill in the refrigerator.
2 Cut up the eggplants into bite-sized pieces. Soak briefly in a bowl of water, drain and pat dry with paper towels. Heat up the frying oil to 340°F (170°C), add the eggplant pieces and deep fry until they turn a darker shade of purple, about 5 minutes.
3 Grate a 4-inch (10-cm) piece of daikon radish. Pour the chilled sauce into 2 small serving bowls, and divide the eggplant and grated daikon radish between the bowls.
4 Cook the somen noodles following the instructions on the packet. Drain well, then rinse in cold running water until completely cool. Drain again. Fill a glass bowl with ice water, and float small bundles of the somen noodles on top. Eat the noodles by dipping them into the sauce and mixing well.

Somen with Walnut Sauce

The nutty fragrance and flavor of the walnuts matches well with the somen noodles. The wasabi then steps in to really brings the flavors into focus.

Serves 2

1¼ cups (300 ml) dashi stock **(see Page 9)**
2 tablespoons rice wine or sake
1½ tablespoons soy sauce
¼ teaspoon of salt
½ teaspoon wasabi paste
15 walnuts
6 oz (175 g) dried somen noodles

1 Put the dashi stock, sake, soy sauce, salt and wasabi paste in a small pan, and bring to a boil over medium heat. Take off the heat and leave to cool to room temperature. Chill in the refrigerator.
2 Grind up the whole walnuts (or 30 halves) with a mortar and pestle. Add the chilled sauce little by little. Transfer the walnut sauce to 2 small serving bowls. Add a sprinkle of chopped walnuts on top.
3 Cook the somen noodles following the instructions on the packet. Drain well, then rinse in cold running water until completely cool. Drain again. Fill a glass bowl with ice water, and float small bundles of the somen noodles on top. Eat the noodles by dipping them into the sauce.

Warm Somen with Seaweed and Sour Plum Sauce

Somen noodles are usually served with a cold sauce, but this version is served with a warm one. The sour-salty flavor of the *umeboshi* (salt-preserved *ume* fruit) becomes quite muted and gentle in this sauce. *Aosa*, also called sea lettuce, is a type of seaweed that's eaten in miso soups. If you can't find it, substitute *aonori* seaweed powder, available at Japanese grocery stores or online.

Serves 2

Scant 2 cups (450 ml) dashi stock (see Page 9)
1 tablespoon mirin or sherry
¼ teaspoon of salt
2 *umeboshi* sour salted plums
1 tablespoon dried *aosa* or *aonori* seaweed, crumbled
1 tablespoon soy sauce
2 tablespoons toasted white sesame seeds
6 oz (175 g) dried somen noodles

1 Put the dashi stock, mirin, salt and *umeboshi* in a small pan, and bring to a boil over medium heat. Turn the heat down to low and add the dried *aosa* or *aonori* seaweed.
2 Bring to a boil, add the soy sauce and transfer to serving bowls. Sprinkle with the toasted white sesame seeds.
3 Cook the somen noodles following the instructions on the packet. Drain well, then rinse in cold running water until completely cool. Drain again. Dip the noodles in the sauce to eat.

....

NOTE As a substitute for the *umeboshi*, dice two fresh plums, mix with 1 teaspoon salt and 2 tablespoons rice vinegar and let sit overnight.

Warm Pork and Soy Milk Somen

This is a somen noodle version of pork and soy milk *shabu shabu*, a popular Japanese hot pot. The key is to not let the soy milk boil.

Serves 2

⅔ cup (150 ml) dashi stock (see Page 9)
2 tablespoons rice wine or sake
1 tablespoon soy sauce
1-inch piece of ginger, peeled and minced
5 oz (150 g) pork loin, cut in eight slices
1¼ cups (300 ml) unsweetened soy milk
½ teaspoon salt
6 oz (175 g) dried somen noodles

1 Put the dashi stock, rice wine/sake, soy sauce and ginger in a small pan, and bring to a boil over medium heat.
2 Separate the slices of pork loin, so they aren't sticking to one another. Add them one at a time to the sauce, and cook while skimming off any fat.
3 Add the unsweetened soy milk, salt and pea shoots to the pan. Turn the heat off just before the pan comes to a boil, and transfer the sauce to serving bowls.
4 Cook the somen noodles following the instructions on the packet. Drain well, then rinse in cold running water until completely cool. Drain again. Dip the noodles in the sauce to eat.

Warm Pork and Soy Milk Somen

Warm Somen with Seaweed and
Sour Plum Sauce

Udon Salad with Tomatoes and Green Shiso

This dish is refreshing yet has plenty of depth of flavor, due to the black vinegar in the sauce.

Serves 2

⅔ cup (150 ml) dashi stock **(see Page 9)**

2 tablespoons rice wine or sake

1½ tablespoons soy sauce

2 tablespoons black vinegar

¼ teaspoon salt

4 small tomatoes, cut in sixths

¼ yellow bell pepper

4 green shiso leaves, or mint or Thai basil

6 oz (175 g) dried udon noodles, or an 8-oz (250-g) package of frozen

1 tablespoon sesame oil

1 Put the dashi stock, sake, soy sauce, black vinegar and salt in a small pan and bring to a boil over medium heat. Cool to room temperature, then chill in the refrigerator.
2 Deseed the bell pepper and slice into thin strips. Roughly chop the green shiso leaves or rip them into small pieces with your hands. Place all the vegetables in a bowl.
3 Prepare the dried or frozen udon noodles following the instructions on the packet. Drain and rinse them under cold running water until they are completely cooled and firm. Drain again and transfer to 2 serving bowls.
4 Add the sesame oil to the chilled sauce. Pour over the noodles. Top the noodles with the vegetables.

Chilled Curry Udon

Curry udon is usually a hot dish, but here I've made a chilled version. Chicken meat retains its light taste even when it's cold, since the fat doesn't become coagulated and heavy.

Serves 2

1 small leek, white part only

2 fresh shiitake mushrooms, trimmed

2 teaspoons sesame oil

1-inch piece of ginger, peeled and minced

Vegetable oil, for frying

5 oz (150 g) ground chicken

1 teaspoon curry powder

1 cup (250 ml) dashi stock **(see Page 9)**

2 tablespoons rice wine or sake

2 tablespoons Japanese curry roux flakes

1 tablespoon soy sauce

6 oz (175 g) dried udon noodles, or an 8-oz (250-g) package of frozen

1-inch piece of ginger, minced

1 Slice the white part of a leek thinly on the diagonal. Slice the mushrooms into quarters.
2 Heat up a pan over medium. Add the sesame oil and ginger and stir fry. When the oil is fragrant, add the ground chicken and curry powder, and stir fry until the meat changes color.
3 Put the leek in the pan and stir fry quickly. Add the dashi stock and rice wine/sake. Bring to a boil while periodically skimming the surface.
4 Add the Japanese curry roux flakes (or 1½ pieces, about 1 oz or 30 g, of curry roux) and the soy sauce to the pan. Bring to a boil then turn off the heat and cool to room temperature. Chill in the refrigerator.
5 Prepare the dried or frozen udon noodles following the instructions on the packet. Drain and rinse them under cold running water until they are completely cooled and firm. Drain again and transfer to 2 serving bowls. Pour the chilled sauce over the noodles, and top with the minced ginger.

Beef Udon

This udon soup is easy to make and a hit with kids as well as adults. Try this for a quick lunch on a weekend.

Serves 2

1 cup (250 ml) dashi stock **(see Page 9)**
1 tablespoon mirin
2 tablespoons soy sauce
5 oz (150 g) thinly sliced raw beef
6 oz (175 g) dried udon noodles, or an 8-oz (250-g) package of frozen
4 green onions, chopped
2 egg yolks

1 Put the seaweed dashi stock, mirin and soy sauce in a pan over medium heat. Bring to a boil.
2 Separate the beef into single slices so they aren't sticking together. Add them to the soup to cook through quickly.
3 Boil two packets of frozen udon noodles following the instructions on the packet. (If you can't find frozen udon noodles, use dried udon noodles, and cook following the instructions on the packet.) Drain the noodles and transfer to 2 serving bowls. Pour the soup over the noodles. Scatter the green onions on the noodles, and top with a raw egg yolk each. (Make sure the eggs are pasteurized or very fresh.)

Yuba and Shirasu Udon

Yuba, also called tofu skin, is a very thin piece of just-set soy milk, and *shirasu* (also called *shirasuboshi*) is whitebait that has been boiled in salted water and semi-dried. Both are available at well-stocked Japanese grocery stores—dried *yuba* in the dry-food section, and *shirasu* in the refrigerated or frozen-food section. Served with udon noodles and a thickened soup, this is a very easy-to-digest, comforting dish even when you don't have much of an appetite.

Serves 2

1/3 oz (10 g) dried *yuba* (tofu skin)
1 cup (250 ml) dashi stock **(see Page 9)**
1 tablespoon soy sauce
1 oz (30 g) shirasu or whitebait
2 teaspoons cornstarch
1 tablespoon water
6 oz (175 g) dried udon noodles, or an 8-oz (250-g) package of frozen
4 green shiso leaves, or mint or Thai basil, cut in ribbons

1 Soak the dried *yuba* in lukewarm water for 5 minutes until it is softened. Drain and cut into bite-sized pieces.
2 Put the dashi stock, soy sauce, *shirasu* and the cut-up *yuba* in a pan over medium heat. Bring to a boil while skimming off any foam. Turn the heat down to low, and simmer for about 5 minutes.
3 Dissolve the cornstarch in the water. Add to the pan to thicken the soup.
4 Boil two packets of frozen udon noodles following the instructions on the packet. (If you can't find frozen udon noodles, use 5½ ounces [160 g] dried udon noodles, and cook following the instructions on the packet.) Drain the noodles and transfer to 2 serving bowls. Pour the soup over the noodles. Finely shred 4 green shiso leaves and put on top of the noodles.

PART 2

Stir-Fried and Pan-Fried Noodles

Pad Thai, Lo Mein, Japchae: These are the famed Asian noodle dishes whose international reputations precede them. Here I've offered my own spin on the crispy pleasures of these fried and familiar favorites. Whether for a quick weeknight meal, next-day noshing or a weekend feast, these heaping treats are sure to make their way into your regular rotation.

Going from Stall to Stall Enjoying Stir-fried Noodles on My Travels!

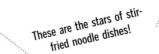

These are the stars of stir-fried noodle dishes!

The recipes featured here are dishes where the noodles are stir fried or pan fried together with other ingredients. From the different types of mi fun or rice vermicelli fried dishes from Taiwan, the variety of lo mein or soft-fried noodles from China, Pad Thai from Thailand to stir-fried glass or cellophane noodles from South Korea, I think that stir-fried noodles also show off the unique characteristics of each country's cuisine. Some stir-fried Asian noodle recipes are made mostly with noodles and not much else, while other dishes include lots of additions. There are also dishes that use cellophane noodles that are strongly flavored and perfect as an accompaniment to plain rice. I could go on and on. Whenever I travel, I always go and eat stir-fried noodles at food stalls. In particular in Bangkok, there are row after row of stalls selling such noodles, and I've spent days on end going from stall to stall sampling their offerings, enticed by the sweet-sour fragrances emanating from them.

Use different combination of noodles and additional ingredients to discover new flavors
For tossed and mixed noodles I prefer simple, straightforward flavors. On the other hand with stir-fried noodles, I like dishes with plenty of additional ingredients. I especially like using lots of my favorite vegetables and greens, and adding umami-rich ingredients like thick deep-fried tofu (*atsuage*) and dried shrimp, and make that kind of stir-fried noodle dish quite often. Stir frying brings out the sweetness of vegetables and the umami in other ingredients. All those flavors are absorbed by the noodles when

HOW TO STIR FRY MI FUN (RICE VERMICELLI)

1 Put the noodles in a bowl, and add enough boiling water to cover. Leave for about 10 minutes until the noodles are softened.

2 Drain the noodles well. If they are long, cut them in half.

3 Stir fry the noodles and other ingredients together, so that the noodles soak up all the flavors of those ingredients.

Long cooking chopsticks are great for moving your noodles, but use whatever tool you prefer when it's time to toss or stir.

Set the mood by serving a mountain of garnishes in baskets like these.

they are combined for delicious results. Another key is to use a tasty, fragrant oil for stir frying, and to add a little bit more than you might normally use. That imparts a depth of flavor.

Stir fries are easy for everyone, and by varying the noodles and added ingredients, it's possible to come up with lots of variations. Please use the recipes in this book as a reference, and discover your own new tasty versions.

Stir-fried mi fun (rice vermicelli) and lo mein continue to grow in popularity

Stir-fried mi fun and lo mein continue to raise their international profiles. Mi fun is a thin noodle made with rice flour, also called rice vermicelli. Banh pho from Vietnam and *sen lek* from Thailand are also made with rice flour, but in Japan rice vermicelli (called *bi-fun* in Japanese)

usually refers to mi fun, the thin noodles used in Chinese and Taiwanese cooking that are similar to a Japanese rice noodle called *harusame*. When making stir-fried dishes using rice vermicelli, make sure the reconstituted noodles soak in plenty of flavor as you stir fry them with the additional ingredients.

When making lo mein, if you can find preboiled or presteamed Chinese noodles you can skip the step of having to boil them before stir frying them. Just untangle the noodles with your hands before pan frying them briefly, then mix in the other ingredients. You can find precooked Chinese noodles labeled as "Hong Kong" or "pan-fried noodles" at Chinese or general Asian grocery stores, and presteamed Chinese noodles labeled as "*yakisoba* noodles" at Japanese grocery stores.

HOW TO STIR FRY PRECOOKED CHINESE NOODLES

1 Gently loosen up the precooked noodles, being careful not to break them.

2 Heat up sesame oil in a frying pan over medium, and add the loosened-up noodles. Stir fry while further untangling the noodles until they are lightly browned.

3 Push the noodles to one side of the frying pan, add the other ingredients to the empty part of the pan and stir fry. When they are cooked through, mix together with the noodles and stir fry a little more.

Stir-Fried Mi Fun with Lots of Vegetables

The crisp-tender shredded vegetables blend well with the thin rice noodles.
You can eat this healthy dish on its own or as an accompaniment to plain rice.

Serves 2

6 oz (175 g) dried rice vermicelli
1 or 2 cabbage leaves
½ carrot
½ onion
1 bunch mustard greens or 4 baby
   bok choi
Sesame oil for stir frying
1-inch piece ginger, peeled and finely
   shredded

Flavorings

3½ tablespoons Shaoxing wine or sake
1 tablespoon fish sauce
2 teaspoons white sesame seeds,
   to garnish

1 Put the rice vermicelli in a bowl, and add enough boiling water to cover. Leave to soak for 10 minutes, then drain well. If the noodles are very long, cut in half.
2 Shred the cabbage and carrots. Slice the onion thinly lengthwise.
3 Cut the greens or bok choi into easy-to-eat pieces.
4 Heat a frying pan over medium. Add 1 tablespoon of sesame oil and the ginger. When the oil smells fragrant, add the cabbage and carrots, and stir fry until they are tender but still crisp.
5 Add the Flavorings to the frying pan and bring to a boil. Add the rice noodles and stir fry so that they absorb the juices from the vegetables *(see photo below)*. When everything is well combined, add the greens or bok choy and 2 teaspoons of sesame oil. Stir fry briefly, and sprinkle with the sesame seeds.

Put the vegetables on the rice noodles, so that you are steaming the noodles with the moisture from the vegetables as you stir fry.

NOTE At diners and food stalls in Taiwan, there are several dishes made with short strands of rice noodles, which are eaten as side dishes with rice rather than standalone noodle dishes. You can vary the vegetables in this recipe, but be sure to always include cabbage, which has lots of moisture to be absorbed by the noodles as you stir fry them, along with lots of flavor.

Spicy Stir-Fried Mi Fun with Gochujang

The rich spiciness of gochujang goes so well with the thin rice noodles.
This is great to nibble on with a beer!

Serves 2

6 oz (175 g) dried rice vermicelli

16 to 20 medium shrimp, about 8 oz
  (220 g)

4 tablespoons cornstarch

6 chives

1 tablespoon sesame oil

1-inch piece of ginger, peeled and thinly
  shredded

1¼ cups (120 g) soybean sprouts,
  trimmed

Flavorings

1 teaspoon gochujang (Korean red chili
  paste)

3½ tablespoons rice wine or sake

2 tablespoons soy sauce

Pinch of salt

1 Put the rice vermicelli in a bowl, and add enough boiling water to cover. Leave to soak for 10 minutes, then drain well. If the noodles are very long, cut in half.

2 Peel the shrimp, cutting into each to remove the vein. Sprinkle with cornstarch, rubbing it in and then rinsing it off. Pat the shrimp dry with paper towels.

3 Cut the chives into 1½ inch (4 cm) long pieces.

4 Heat a frying pan over medium, and add the sesame oil and ginger. When the oil is fragrant, add the noodles and stir fry while loosening them up.

5 Add the combined Flavorings to the pan, and stir fry the noodles while they absorb the liquid. Add the shrimp and stir fry until cooked through, about 3 to 4 minutes. Add the chives and bean sprouts, and stir fry briefly.

. . . .

NOTE One of the great things about stir-fried mi fun is that you can vary it so much by changing up the added ingredients. Here I have used Korean gochujang and made it a bit spicy. You can use *doubanjiang*, a spicy bean paste from Sichuan Province in China, instead, but I prefer to use gochujang since it is slightly sweet.

Seafood Stir-Fried Mi Fun with Fresh Clams

The flavors from the seafood and the oyster sauce are soaked up by the rice noodles, while the garlic scapes add texture and kick to the dish.

Serves 2

6 oz (175 g) dried rice vermicelli
1 small fresh squid
2 stalks garlic scapes or garlic shoots
1 tablespoon sesame oil
1 clove garlic, peeled and sliced thin
1-inch piece of unpeeled ginger, finely shredded
7 oz (200 g) fresh Manila or littleneck clams, in shells, cleaned and soaked in salted water to remove grit
Chili pepper flakes, to taste

Flavorings

2 tablespoons oyster sauce
2 tablespoons rice wine or sake
1 tablespoon black vinegar
1 teaspoon soy sauce

1 Put the rice vermicelli in a bowl, and add enough boiling water to cover. Leave to soak for 10 minutes, then drain well. If the noodles are very long, cut in half.
2 Remove the legs, cartilage and innards from the squid, and peel off the thin skin. Rinse under running water and pat dry. Cut the body open lengthwise, and slice into ⅓ inch (1 cm) wide strips.
3 Cut the garlic scapes into about 1 inch (3 cm) long pieces.
4 Heat a frying pan over medium. Add ½ tablespoon of sesame oil, the garlic and ginger, and stir fry briefly. Add the noodles and stir fry while loosening them up.
5 Add the garlic scapes and the combined Flavorings and stir fry, letting the noodles absorb the flavors. When the liquid in the frying pan has been reduced by half, add the squid and the clams and stir fry briefly. Reduce the heat to low, cover with a lid and steam-cook until the clams open up, about 3 minutes.
6 Turn the heat back up to medium and mix in the rest of the sesame oil. Transfer to serving plates, and sprinkle with the chili pepper flakes.

....

NOTE Seafood mi fun is seen frequently in southern China, where there are a lot of seafood dishes. Here I've added oyster sauce to the delicious liquid that comes out of the clams to make this a dish packed with the flavors of the sea.

Stir-Fried Mi Fun with Ground Pork and Bean Sprouts

The fragrance of the five-spice powder makes me feel like I'm back in Taiwan. The key to this dish is to add the bean sprouts at the last minute to preserve their crispy texture.

Serves 2

6 oz (175 g) dried rice vermicelli
1 red bell pepper
1 tablespoon sesame oil
1 clove garlic, peeled and finely shredded
1-inch piece of unpeeled ginger, finely shredded
4 oz (120 g) ground pork
1¼ cups (120 g) soybean sprouts, trimmed

Flavorings
½ teaspoon five-spice powder
3 tablespoons rice wine or sake
2 tablespoons fish sauce

1 Put the rice vermicelli in a bowl, and add enough boiling water to cover. Leave to soak for 10 minutes, then drain well. If the noodles are very long, cut in half.

2 Remove the seeds from the bell peppers and slice thinly lengthwise.

3 Heat a frying pan over medium. Add the sesame oil, the garlic and ginger. When the oil is fragrant add the pork, and stir fry until it changes color.

4 Add the noodles and stir fry while loosening them up. Add the combined Flavorings and stir fry so that the liquid is absorbed by the noodles. Add the bean sprouts *(see photo below)*, and stir fry briefly.

NOTE This is a stir-fried mi fun dish that you can make very quickly. The five-spice powder really adds a touch of authentic Chinese flavor to this dish.

Add the bean sprouts at the last minute and stir fry them quickly to preserve their crispy texture.

Shanghainese Stir-Fried Noodles with Pork and Vegetables

The oyster sauce clings to the springy noodles in this rich dish featuring tangy mustard greens.

Serves 2

6 oz (175 g) thinly sliced pork
1 bunch mustard greens or 2 baby bok choi
10 oz (300 g) fresh *mee pok* or 7 oz (200 g) dried thin wheat noodles
4 teaspoons sesame oil
1 clove garlic, peeled and minced

Flavorings
2 tablespoons oyster sauce
3½ tablespoons rice wine or sake
2 teaspoons soy sauce

1 Slice the pork into thin strips.
2 Cut up the mustard greens or bok choi into easy-to-eat pieces.
3 Cook the noodles following the instructions on the packet. Drain well, then rinse in several changes of cold water until the noodles don't feel sticky. Drain well again.
4 Heat 2 teaspoons of sesame oil and the garlic in a frying pan over medium. When the oil is fragrant, add the pork and stir fry until it changes color.
5 Add the drained noodles and the combined Flavorings **(see photo below)**, and stir fry until there is very little moisture left in the frying pan. When everything is well-mixed, add the rest of the sesame oil.

....

NOTE Thick wheat noodles are the norm, as well as the use of a sweet Chinese soy sauce. Here I have used *mee pok* noodles, and used both soy sauce and oyster sauce to add the rich deep flavor that characterizes the original.

Add the well-rinsed noodles to the frying pan after the pork has been cooked, and stir fry.

Stir-Fried Ramen with Chives, Ginger and Scallops

This stir-fried noodle dish is a great way to enjoy the refined flavor and subtle sweetness of yellow Chinese chives. The umami of the scallops really stands out, and is so delicious!

Serves 2

2 packets precooked ramen noodles, about 10 oz (300 g) total
8 large fresh or frozen scallops, about 7 oz (200 g) total
1 leek, white part only
10 stalks yellow Chinese chives or 1 bunch regular chives
1 tablespoon sesame oil
1-inch piece of unpeeled ginger, finely shredded
Freshly grated black pepper to taste

Flavorings

2 tablespoons rice wine or sake
2 tablespoons fish sauce

1 Quarter the scallops. Slice the leek thinly on the diagonal.

2 Cut the yellow Chinese chives into 1½ inch (4 cm) long pieces.

3 Heat a frying pan over medium heat and add the sesame oil and ginger. When the oil is fragrant, add the noodles to the pan and stir fry while loosening them.

4 When the noodles are well-coated with oil, add the scallops and the combined Flavorings, and stir fry the scallops about 3 minutes. Add the Chinese chives and stir fry quickly. Transfer to the plates, adding black pepper to taste.

....

NOTE Yellow Chinese chives are blanched as they grow so that they are yellow instead of green, and very tender and sweet, like Chinese asparagus. They are used a lot in Chinese cooking. I have kept the flavors simple, using just rice wine/sake and fish sauce to enhance the sweetness of the chives. You can find yellow Chinese chives at well-stocked Asian or Chinese groceries. You can use thinly sliced pork instead of the scallops.

Shanghai-Style Hot Sauce Noodles Lajiang Mian

The fragrant sesame chili oil adds just enough spiciness to this delicious stir-fried noodle dish. The textures of the leek and king oyster mushrooms especially complement the noodles.

Serves 2

6 oz (175 g) ground pork
1 leek, white part only
2 king oyster mushrooms
1 tablespoon sesame oil
1 garlic clove, peeled and finely shredded
2 tablespoons rice wine or sake
8 oz (250 g) fresh Chinese lo mein
  noodles

Flavorings
2 teaspoons sesame chili oil
2 tablespoons soy sauce
1/4 teaspoon salt

1 Slice the leek thinly on the diagonal. Cut the king oyster mushrooms in half lengthwise, then cut into 1/4 inch (6 mm) thick slices.

2 Heat the sesame oil and garlic in a frying pan over medium. When the oil is fragrant, add the ground pork, and stir fry until the meat changes color. Add the leek, mushrooms and sake, and continue stir frying until the vegetables turn limp.

3 Cook the fresh Chinese noodles following the instructions on the packet. (If there are no instructions: bring a generous amount of water to a boil in a large pan. Add the noodles, and cook for 2 to 3 minutes, testing for doneness.) Drain well, then add to the pan and stir fry while untangling them. Add the combined Flavorings and stir fry until they are absorbed by the noodles and vegetables.

....

NOTE *Lajiang mian* is usually a spicy noodle soup, but here I have used the flavors of a noodle dish I had at a Chinese restaurant as inspiration to come up with this stir-fried version. Adjust the amount of sesame chili oil to taste.

Bean Sprout and Zha Cai Stir-Fried Noodles

Zha cai, a type of Chinese pickle made with kohlrabi, is combined with bean sprouts and pea shoots for a dish that's simple yet has complex flavors. It's easily made with precooked Chinese noodles.

Serves 2

1¼ cups (120 g) soybean sprouts, trimmed

¼ cup (30 g) Chinese *zha cai* pickles, pickled mustard greens or sauerkraut

1 leek, white part only

½ cup (45 g) pea shoots

1 tablespoon sesame oil

1-inch piece of ginger, peeled and finely shredded

2 packets precooked Chinese noodles, about 10 oz (300 g) total

2 teaspoons toasted white sesame seeds, to garnish

Flavorings

2 tablespoons Shaoxing wine or pale dry sherry

½ teaspoon salt

1 Slice the *zha cai* thinly, and soak in cold water for about 8 minutes to remove some of the salt. Drain and shred finely. Slice the leek thinly on the diagonal.

2 Trim the ends of the pea shoots, and then cut in half.

3 Heat a frying pan over medium and add the sesame oil and ginger. When the oil is fragrant, add the noodles and stir fry while loosening them up. Push them to one side and add the *zha cai* and leek. Stir fry briefly, then mix in.

4 Add the Flavorings, pea shoots and bean sprouts. Stir fry briefly. Transfer to serving plates and sprinkle with the sesame seeds.

....

NOTE *Zha cai* is a very popular pickle in China. Pea shoots are also becoming increasingly popular, but use whatever sprout or shoot is available or the type you prefer. The flavors of this stir-fried noodle dish are brought together by adding Shaoxing wine.

Stir-Fried Glass Noodles with Scallops and Eggs

Mix the yolk of the fried egg with the rest of the ingredients before eating this treat! Don't forget to toss in the peanuts, which add a great accent.

Serves 2

5 oz (150 g) dried glass or cellophane noodles
7 sprigs fresh cilantro
1 tablespoon sesame oil
2 eggs
1 clove garlic, peeled and minced
12 to 14 medium fresh scallops, about 8 oz (225 g) total
2 tablespoons peanuts, roughly chopped
Freshly ground black pepper to taste

Flavorings

2 tablespoons rice wine or sake
2 tablespoons fish sauce

1 Bring a pot of water to a boil. Add the glass noodles and cook for 90 seconds. Drain.
2 Chop up the cilantro roughly.
3 Heat up the sesame oil in a frying pan over medium. Break in the eggs and make 2 fried eggs sunny side up with soft-set yolks. Take out the eggs.
4 Add the garlic to the frying pan and cook over medium heat. When the oil is fragrant, add the drained noodles and the scallops, and stir fry while loosening up the noodles until the scallops are cooked through.
5 Add the Flavorings, and stir fry until there is very little liquid left in the pan. Add the cilantro. Transfer to serving plates and top with the fried eggs. Scatter on the peanuts and sprinkle with black pepper.

Stir-Fried Noodles with Water Spinach & Fish Sauce

This dish is simply flavored with sake and fish sauce. Add spiciness with red chili pepper and sourness with lime juice.

Serves 2

5 oz (150 g) thinly sliced pork
8 stalks water spinach (seri or kangkong), or watercress
5 oz (150 g) dried thin rice noodles
1 tablespoon sesame oil
1 clove garlic, peeled and finely chopped
1-inch piece of ginger, peeled and finely chopped
½ red Thai chili or serrano pepper, deseeded and chopped
2 lime wedges, to serve

Flavorings

2 tablespoons rice wine or sake
2 tablespoons fish sauce

1 Slice the pork into ⅓ inch (1 cm) wide strips.
2 Cut up the water spinach into easy-to-eat pieces.
3 Cook the rice noodles following the instructions on the packet. Drain well.
4 Heat up a frying pan over medium. Add the sesame oil, the garlic and ginger. When the oil is fragrant, add the pork, and stir fry until it changes color.
5 Add the chili pepper and the noodles to the pan, and stir fry while loosening up the noodles. Add the Flavorings and continue stir frying until the liquid is absorbed by the noodles. Add the water spinach and stir fry briefly. Transfer to a serving plate, and serve with the lime wedges.

NOTE This stir-fried noodle dish is available from many food stalls in Thailand. Despite the image Thai food has of being spicy, this is not spicy at all. It has lots of ingredients like shrimp, bean sprouts and eggs, but the key is the flavorful tofu and the crunchy texture of the daikon radish pickles.

A You can't leave out umami-rich ingredients like dried shrimp, daikon radish pickles and deep-fried tofu.

B Add the cooked and well-drained rice noodles (*sen lek*) after the other ingredients with the flavors have been stir fried.

Pad Thai with Shrimp

This dish is packed with umami-rich ingredients, and is guaranteed to be tasty! The slippery texture of the *sen lek* rice noodles is part of the appeal.

Serves 2

¼ cup (20 g) small dried shrimp
8 to 10 medium fresh shrimp, about 4 oz (120 g) total
2 tablespoons cornstarch
8 oz (225 g) thick deep-fried tofu
½ cup (50 g) pickled daikon radish (optional)
1 tablespoon sesame oil
1 bunch chives
2 eggs, beaten
5 oz (150 g) thin dried rice noodles
1¼ cups (120 g) soybean sprouts, trimmed

Flavorings

2 tablespoons rice wine or sake
2 tablespoons fish sauce

1 Soak the dried shrimp in 4 tablespoons of lukewarm water for about 20 minutes to soften. Chop coarsely, reserving the soaking liquid.
2 Peel the fresh shrimp, leaving the tails on. Remove the veins. Sprinkle with cornstarch, rub it into the shrimp and then rinse off (this cleans the shrimp). Pat the shrimp dry with paper towels.
3 Cut the fried tofu into ⅔ inch (1.5 cm) cubes. Chop the pickled daikon roughly. Cut the chives into about 1 inch (3 cm) long pieces **(see photo A)**.
4 Heat up ½ tablespoon of sesame oil in a frying pan over medium. Pour in the beaten eggs and mix. When they are soft-set, remove the eggs from the pan.
5 Cook the rice noodles following the instructions on the packet.
6 Add the rest of the sesame oil along with the dried shrimp, the soaking liquid, fried tofu, pickled daikon, shrimp and the combined Flavorings. Stir fry briefly.
7 Add the rice noodles to the frying pan **(see photo B)** and stir fry while loosening them up. Cover the pan with a lid and steam-cook for 3 minutes. Add the bean sprouts, chives and scrambled eggs, and mix everything together.

Vietnamese Stir-Fried Beef Noodles

This dish is unusual in that it's made with wheat flour or Chinese-style noodles rather than the rice noodles that are more commonly used in Vietnam. Stir frying is what gives the dish its signature taste.

1 Slice the onion thinly lengthwise (with the grain). Cut the carrot into thin strips.
2 Roughly chop the cilantro.
3 Heat up ½ tablespoon of sesame oil and the garlic in a frying pan over medium. When the oil is fragrant add the beef, onion and carrot, and stir fry until the meat changes color. Add the Flavorings and mix well.
4 Cook the noodles following the instructions on the packet. (If there are no instructions, bring a generous amount of water to a boil in a large pan. Add the noodles, and cook for 2 to 3 minutes, testing for doneness.) Drain well and add to the pan, stir frying while loosening the noodles up. Add the rest of the sesame oil and the cilantro/coriander, and stir fry quickly. Sprinkle with the sesame seeds.

Serves 2

½ onion
½ carrot
6 sprigs fresh cilantro (coriander leaves)
1 tablespoon sesame oil
1 clove garlic, peeled and minced
5 oz (150 g) thinly sliced beef
8 oz (240 g) fresh Chinese lo mein
   noodles
2 teaspoons toasted white sesame seeds,
   to garnish

Flavorings

2 tablespoons oyster sauce
2 tablespoons Shaoxing wine or sake
2 tablespoons fish sauce

Vietnamese Rice Noodles (Bun) with Beef and Basil

The thin rice noodles and the flavorful beef go together exceptionally well. With the addition of basil, this has very Vietnamese flavors.

Serves 2

½ red onion
1 tablespoon sesame oil
1 clove garlic, peeled and crushed
5 oz (150 g) thinly sliced beef
5 oz (150 g) dried rice vermicelli
2 sprigs of Thai basil
½ lemon, to serve

Flavorings

2 tablespoons rice wine or sake
2 tablespoons fish sauce

1 Slice the red onion thinly lengthwise.
2 Heat up the sesame oil and garlic in a frying pan over medium. When the oil is fragrant, add the beef and the onion, and stir fry until the meat changes color.
3 Cook the rice vermicelli (bun) following the instructions on the packet. Drain.
4 Add the Flavorings to the frying pan and mix well. Add the noodles, and stir fry while loosening them up. Transfer to serving plates. Top with the basil leaves, and squeeze on the lemon.

Korean Stir-Fried Glass Noodles with Beef Ribs Japchae

This is one of Korea's signature dishes, appearing in many guises on menus around the world.

Serves 2

5 oz (150 g) boneless beef ribs
½ carrot
4 thin green onions
5 oz (150 g) dried glass or cellophane noodles (dangmyeon)
1 tablespoon sesame oil
2 teaspoons toasted white sesame seeds

Flavorings

1 clove garlic, peeled and minced
1-inch piece of ginger, peeled and grated
2 tablespoons rice wine or sake
1 tablespoon mirin or sherry
1½ tablespoons soy sauce

1 Slice the beef and carrot into ¼ inch (7-8 mm) wide strips.
2 Cut the green onions into 2 inch (5 cm) long pieces.
3 Cook the glass noodles following the instructions on the packet.
4 Heat up the sesame oil in a frying pan over medium. Add the beef and carrots and stir fry until the beef changes color. Add the Flavorings and bring to a boil.
5 Add the noodles, and stir fry while letting them absorb the liquid in the pan. Add the green onions and stir fry quickly. Transfer to serving plates and sprinkle with the sesame seeds.

Stir-Fried Noodles with Kimchi and Dried Fish

Dried fish is used frequently in Korean cooking to make soup stock, just as it is in Japanese cooking. This tastes rather like fast food, and you'll want to eat it again and again.

Serves 2

½ cup (80 g) chopped cabbage kimchi
1 leek, white part only
8 to 10 medium-sized dried whitebait
7 oz (200 g) dried Chinese wheat noodles
1 tablespoon sesame oil
Coarsely ground red chili pepper, to taste

Flavorings

2 tablespoons rice wine or sake
1 tablespoon soy sauce

1 Chop the kimchi up roughly. Cut the leek into 1½ inch (4cm) long pieces, then slice each piece in half lengthwise.
2 Remove the heads and guts from the dried fish, and split in half lengthwise. Place a frying pan over medium heat, add the fish and dry-roast them for 1 to 2 minutes.
3 Cook the noodles following the instructions. Drain well.
4 Add the sesame oil to the frying pan along with the kimchi and leek, and stir fry until the leek is limp. Add the noodles and the Flavorings and stir fry. Transfer to serving plates, and sprinkle with the coarsely ground red chili pepper.

Shrimp Roe Noodles

Shrimp roe noodles, a specialty of Hong Kong and Macau, are usually made with shrimp roe on the noodles. Here I have used stir-fried shrimp and paired them with dried shrimp roe noodles where the shrimp roe is kneaded into the dough.

Serves 2

7 oz (200 g) peeled and cleaned medium shrimp
2 tablespoons cornstarch
4 green onions
1-inch piece of ginger, peeled and finely shredded
1 tablespoon sesame oil
6 oz (150 g) dried shrimp roe noodles
1 cup (100 g) soybean sprouts, trimmed

Flavorings

2 tablespoons Shaoxing wine or sake
1 tablespoon black vinegar
1 tablespoon soy sauce

1 Sprinkle the shrimp with cornstarch and rub it in well. Rinse the starch off (this cleans the shrimp). Pat the shrimp dry with paper towels, and chop up roughly.
2 Cut the green onions into ¾ inch (2 cm) pieces.
3 Heat up a frying pan over medium. Add ½ tablespoon of sesame oil and the ginger. When the oil is fragrant, add the shrimp and stir fry until they change color.
4 Cook the shrimp roe noodles following the instructions on the packet. Drain well. Add to the pan with the Flavorings, and stir fry while loosening the noodles up.
5 Add the bean sprouts and the green onions and stir fry. Swirl in the rest of the sesame oil.

Stir-Fried Noodles with Bamboo Shoots, Pork and Oyster Sauce

The combination of the rich flavor of the oyster sauce and the deep fragrance of the black vinegar makes this a quintessential Chinese-style noodle dish.

1 Cut the pork into bite-sized pieces.
2 Drain the bamboo shoots and cut into thin slices. Cut the garlic shoots into ¾ inch (2 cm) pieces.
3 Heat up a frying pan over medium. Add ½ tablespoon of sesame oil, the ginger and bean paste (*doubanjiang*) and stir fry. When the oil is fragrant, add the pork, and stir fry until it changes color.
4 Cook the noodles following the instructions on the packet. (If there are no instructions, bring a generous amount of water to a boil in a large pan. Add the noodles, and cook for 2 to 3 minutes, testing for doneness.) Drain well.
5 Add the bamboo shoots and garlic shoots to the frying pan and stir fry. Add the Flavorings and bring to a boil. Add the noodles and stir fry while loosening them up. Swirl in the rest of the sesame oil.

Serves 2

5 oz (150 g) thinly sliced pork loin
1 cup (120 g) precooked bamboo shoots, vacuum packed or canned
4 garlic shoots or 1 bunch garlic chives
1 tablespoon sesame oil
1-inch piece of ginger, peeled and finely shredded
¾ teaspoon spicy Sichuan bean paste (doubanjiang)
8 oz (240 g) fresh Chinese lo mein noodles

Flavorings
2 tablespoons oyster sauce
2 tablespoons Shaoxing wine
1 tablespoon black vinegar
Pinch of salt

PART 3
Soup Noodles

Soup noodles seem to have taken the world by storm! In this section you'll find such delights as pho from Vietnam, Thai noodle soups, *naengmyeon* (cold noodle soup) from Korea and of course *dan dan* noodles from China. There's plenty of choice here for steaming bowls of soup noodles that you can enjoy throughout the year.

Everyone Loves a Comforting Bowl of Soup Noodles

The texture and mouthfeel of the noodles is especially important in these dishes.

Asian soup noodle dishes are often very light, easy to eat and comforting. They are gently flavored and are not too spicy or heavy, so if you're cooking for a crowd, everyone is able to enjoy soup noodles. They combine substance and lightness in one bowl, the best of both worlds.

The recipes I'm introducing to you in this chapter include many such gently flavored, easy-to-eat dishes. In particular, the different types of pho from Vietnam (see Pages 58-61, 64), Khao Soi from Thailand (see Page 62) and *ta-a* or *danzi* noodles from Taiwan (see Page 71) are lightly salted and quite refreshing. In addition, pho and Khao Soi turn to slippery rice noodles for their texture and versatility. The soups rely on the flavors of the vegetables and meat, so they are very gentle on your stomach and go perfectly with the noodles.

Toppings and condiments create new flavors
As is the case with the tossed and mixed noodles in Part 1, you can enjoy adding your own mix of toppings and condiments to soup noodles. Or add *shichimi togarashi* (seven-flavor chili powder), sansho pepper and so on if you're using soba or udon noodles. The simpler the noodle dish, the more you can vary its flavors by adding hotness with chili sauce or chili peppers, refreshing tanginess with lime or lemon juice, rich umami with fish sauces such as *nam*

HOW TO COOK RICE NOODLES

1 Bring a generous amount of water (the rule of thumb is 4½ cups or 1 liter per 2⅔ ounces or 8 grams of pho) to a boil. When the water is at a full boil, add the pho.

2 Let the pho cook for a few seconds, until they loosen up. Cook further while stirring following the directions on the packet (usually 4 to 5 minutes).

3 Once the pho is cooked, drain immediately. Shake off any excess water well.

I love collecting pretty porcelain soup spoons.

I use dishes I buy during my travels to serve condiments and garnishes. It really perks up the dining table.

pla and *nuoc mam,* sweetness with sugar and so on—that's the most appealing part of eating Asian noodles.

In addition, when you travel around various Asian countries you will often encounter local people slurping down soup noodles for breakfast. In Japan, we like to have miso soup in the morning to get the day off to a good start, but in other Asian countries soup noodles may be the soul food that gives them energy.

Rice noodles such as pho and glass noodles
Banh pho is a Vietnamese noodle that's made with rice flour. It's very popular since it's slippery and so adaptable, and in this book I've used it in tossed noodle dishes as well as soup noodles. Pho has become so popular in the West—and the rest of the non-Asian world—that the noodles are much easier to buy than in the past. Glass or cellophane noodles made with mung bean flour are also commonly used in soup noodle recipes. Here I've included a recipe for Mien Ga from Vietnam (see Page 67). These noodles are lighter than noodles made with wheat or rice flour, so I recommend them when you don't have much of an appetite, or are looking for a light meal. Both pho and cellophane noodles are cooked in plenty of water, just like other noodles. Please be sure to drain them well after they're done.

HOW TO COOK MUNG BEAN GLASS OR CELLOPHANE NOODLES

1 Bring a generous amount of water (the rule of thumb is 4½ cups or 1 liter per 2 ounces or 6 grams of glass noodles). When the water is at a full boil, add the glass noodles.

2 Let the noodles cook for a few seconds until they loosen up. Cook further while stirring following the directions on the packet (usually around 2 minutes).

3 Once the noodles are cooked, drain immediately. Shake off any excess water well.

Beef Pho Noodle Soup

The thinly sliced rare beef in this dish is exceptionally delicious with the broth! The watercress and peanuts also enhance the flavor of the rice flour noodles.

Serves 2

½ onion
4 oz (120 g) thinly sliced beef round
6 oz (175 g) dried flat rice noodles
1 bunch watercress
2 tablespoons freshly squeezed lemon
  juice
2 tablespoons chopped peanuts

Soup

2½ cups (600 ml) beef stock with
  ½ teaspoon of five-spice powder
1-inch piece of unpeeled ginger,
  thinly sliced
2 tablespoons rice wine or sake
2½ tablespoons fish sauce

1 Slice the onion thinly lengthwise.
2 Put the Soup ingredients and the onions in a pan, and start heating over medium. When it comes to a boil, turn the heat down to low, cover with a lid and simmer for about 5 minutes. Separate the beef slices so they aren't sticking to one another. Add them to the Soup one slice at a time **(see photo below)** and cook for about 1 minute. Remove the beef from the soup, and skim the foam off the top.
3 Cook the noodles following the instructions on the packet. Drain well, and transfer to serving bowls. Pour on the Soup and add the beef. Roughly chop the watercress and put on top of the noodles. Add the lemon juice and scatter on the peanuts.

NOTE *Banh pho* is a noodle made with rice flour that is indispensable to Vietnamese cuisine. Beef pho is one of the best-known dishes made with this noodle. In Vietnam this pho is made with beef stock, so I've tried to replicate those flavors here.

Separate the beef into single slices, and heat through quickly so that they are still tender and rare.

Seafood Pho Noodle Soup Pho Ngheu

Pho made with a clam-flavored soup is very fragrant and different. Sliced red onions and fresh herbs add a refreshing flavor and more depth.

Serves 2

½ red onion

10 oz (300 g) fresh littlencck clams, in shells, cleaned and soaked in salted water to remove grit

6 oz (175 g) dried flat rice noodles

1 cup (20 g) combined fresh mint and Thai basil leaves

2 lime wedges

Soup

2½ cups (600 ml) dashi stock **(see Page 9)**

1-inch piece of unpeeled ginger, thinly sliced

2 tablespoons rice wine or sake

2½ tablespoons fish sauce

1 Slice the red onion thinly lengthwise. Put the slices into a bowl of cold water for 5 minutes. Drain well.

2 Put the Soup ingredients in a pan over medium heat. When it comes to a boil, add the clams. Bring to a boil while skimming the surface. Turn the heat down to low, cover the pan with a lid, and simmer for about 5 minutes.

3 Cook the noodles following the instructions on the packet. Drain well, and transfer to serving bowls. Pour on the Soup and clams, top with the mint and basil leaves, and squeeze on the lime.

....

NOTE Besides the usual beef and chicken pho, seafood pho recipes are also popular. This clam pho dish is called *pho ngheu*. The soup is very light and elegant when compared to beef or chicken pho, and the noodles are so slippery and easy to slurp.

Chicken Pho Noodle Soup

The chicken broth that fills the bowl is so delicious, you'll want to just drink it right up!
The crispy texture and fragrance of the raw bean sprouts is also key.

Serves 2

7 oz (150 g) boneless chicken thighs
6 oz (175 g) dried flat rice noodles
1¼ cups (120 g) soybean sprouts, trimmed
4 green onions, sliced diagonally into 1 inch
 (about 3 cm) long pieces
6 sprigs fresh cilantro (coriander leaves)
2 lemon wedges

Soup

2½ cups (600 ml) chicken stock
1-inch piece of unpeeled ginger, thinly sliced
2 tablespoons rice wine sake
2½ tablespoons fish sauce

1 Optionally remove the skin from the chicken thigh meat. Cut the chicken into bite-sized pieces.

2 Put the Soup ingredients in a pan over medium heat. When it comes to a boil, add the cut-up chicken, and bring back to a boil while skimming off any fat. Turn the heat down to low, cover with a lid and simmer for about 8 minutes.

3 Cook the noodles following the instructions on the packet. Drain well, and transfer to serving bowls. Pour the Soup and chicken into the bowls. Put the bean sprouts, green onions and cilantro on the noodles, and squeeze the lemon over them.

....

NOTE Called *pho ga*, chicken pho is as popular in Vietnam as the beef version. Both types of pho are adjusted by diners to their own tastes by adding vegetables and herbs or squeezing on lemon juice. Eating bean sprouts raw is also very typically Vietnamese.

Vegetable Pho Noodle Soup

This is a very refreshing soup that hightlights the acidity of tomato. The fried onion is also terrific in this punchy veggie version of pho.

Serves 2

¾ cup (120 g) broccoli florets
10 cherry tomatoes
1 tablespoon lime juice
6 oz (170 g) dried flat rice noodles
4 lettuce leaves, shredded

Soup
2½ cups (600 ml) vegetable stock
1-inch piece of unpeeled ginger, thinly sliced
2 tablespoons rice wine or sake
2½ tablespoons fish sauce

Fried Onions
½ onion
Oil for deep frying

1 Make the fried onions. Slice the onion, and place the slices on a flat sieve or colander. Leave for 1 to 2 hours. Deep fry the onion slices in 320°F (160°C) oil until golden brown *(see photo)*. Drain.
2 Divide the broccoli into small florets. Remove the stems from the tomatoes.
3 Put the broccoli, tomatoes and Soup ingredients in a pan over medium heat. Bring to a boil while skimming off any foam. Turn the heat down to low, cover with a lid and simmer for about 2 minutes. Add the lime juice.
4 Cook the noodles following the instructions on the packet. Drain well, and transfer to serving bowls. Pour the Soup and vegetables over the noodles. Top with the shredded lettuce and 2 tablespoons each of the Fried Onions.

Onion slices that have been allowed to dry fry up to a deep golden brown, and turn very sweet.

NOTE In Vietnam and Thailand, deep-fried onions are used a lot in cooking. Here I have used them in a vegetable-only pho to add richness. You can add fried onions to dishes other than pho, such as salads and other soups when you want to add something extra. They keep for 4 to 5 days, so you can make them in quantity.

Thai Curry Noodle Soup Khao Soi

The harmonious combination of the spices and fish sauce is habit-forming.

Serves 2

5 oz (150 g) pork
½ red onion
1 teaspoon sesame oil
1-inch piece of ginger, peeled and minced
1½ teaspoons curry powder

....

NOTE This curry noodle soup is eaten in northern Thailand and Laos. Some versions include coconut milk or are topped with deep-fried noodles.

2½ tablespoons fish sauce
6 oz (175 g) dried thin rice noodles
5 sprigs watercress, roughly chopped
2 slices lemon
Additional curry powder to taste

Soup
½ green Thai chili or serrano pepper, chopped
3 tablespoons rice wine or sake
2 cups plus 2 tablespoons (500 ml) water

1 Cut the pork and onion into ⅓ inch (1 cm) cubes.
2 Heat a pan over medium. Add the sesame oil, ginger and curry powder. When the oil is fragrant, add the pork and onion, and stir fry until the pork changes color.
3 Add the Soup ingredients to the pan and bring to a boil while skimming off the top. Turn the heat down to low, cover with a lid and simmer for about 8 minutes. Add the fish sauce, taste and add more if needed.
4 Cook the noodles following the instructions on the packet. Drain well and transfer to serving bowls. Pour the Soup over the noodles, top with the watercress and lemon, and sprinkle with some curry powder.

Thai Lemongrass Noodles with Spare Ribs

The teaming of the strong meat stock that comes from the spare ribs and the flavor of the lemongrass is what really sets this dish apart!

Serves 2

2 teaspoons sesame oil

1 clove garlic, peeled and thinly sliced

1-inch piece of unpeeled ginger, thinly sliced

14 oz (400 g) pork spare ribs, bone-in

2½ tablespoons fish sauce

6 oz (175 g) dried thin rice noodles

3 green onions, sliced diagonally into 1 inch (3 cm) long pieces

2 slices lemon

Soup

1 dried 2-inch (5-cm) square piece *kombu* seaweed

4 stalks lemongrass

1 kaffir lime leaf or 1½ teaspoons grated lime zest`

3 to 4 small Thai chili peppers, or 2 serrano peppers

½ cup (110 ml) rice wine or sake

3½ cups (800 ml) water

1 Heat up a pan over medium and add the sesame oil, garlic and ginger. When the oil is fragrant, add the spare ribs and brown.

2 Add the Soup ingredients and bring to a boil while skimming off the top. Turn the heat down to low, cover with a lid and simmer for about 50 minutes. Add the fish sauce, taste and add more if needed.

3 Cook the noodles following the directions on the packet. Drain well, and transfer to serving bowls. Pour on the Soup and spare ribs. Top with the green onions and lemon.

....

NOTE This is a noodle version of a Thai spare rib soup. If you simmer the ribs with lemongrass and chili peppers, you can eliminate the gaminess of the pork.

Rich Bone Shank Pho

This umami-rich soup made with simmered beef, coriander roots, garlic and ginger is absolutely delicious!

Serves 2

10 oz (300 g) beef shank with the bone
1 tablespoon fish sauce
1½ tablespoons soy sauce
7 oz (150 g) dried flat rice noodles
1 sprig fresh cilantro (coriander leaves)

Soup

2 fresh coriander roots, cut in half lengthwise
1 clove garlic, peeled and crushed
1-inch piece of unpeeled ginger, thinly sliced
¼ cup (45 ml) rice wine or sake
5 cups (1.2 l) water

1 Put the Soup ingredients in a pan over medium heat. When it comes to a boil, add the beef and bring back to a boil while skimming off the surface. Turn the heat down to low, cover with a lid and simmer for about 50 minutes. Add the fish sauce and soy sauce.
2 Cook the noodles following the instructions on the packet. Drain well and transfer to serving bowls.
3 Shred the cooked beef and put on top of the noodles. Pour on the Soup, and top with the fresh cilantro.

Shrimp Tom Yum

Coconut milk is added to a broth packed with the umami of shrimp and the fragrance of lemongrass in this very Thai-flavored noodle soup.

Serves 2

8 large fresh shrimp, about 5 oz (150 g) total
2 tablespoons cornstarch
⅔ cup (50 g) shiitake or enoki mushrooms
2 medium red bell peppers
1 cup (235 ml) coconut milk
2½ tablespoons fish sauce
8 oz (240 g) fresh Chinese lo mein noodles
Freshly ground black pepper to taste

Soup

1⅔ cups (400 ml) dashi stock (see Page 9)
3 to 4 stalks lemongrass
½ red Thai chili or serrano pepper (cut in half lengthwise), deseeded
2 tablespoons rice wine or sake

1 Shell and devein the shrimp. Sprinkle with potato or cornstarch and rub well, then rinse under running water (this cleans the shrimp). Pat dry with paper towels.
2 Cut the ends off the mushrooms and divide into small clumps. Remove the seeds from the bell peppers and slice thinly lengthwise.
3 Put the Soup ingredients in a pan over medium heat and bring to a boil. Add the shrimp, mushrooms and bell peppers, and bring back to a boil while skimming off the top. Turn the heat down to low, cover with a lid and simmer for about 5 minutes. Add the coconut milk and fish sauce.
4 Cook the noodles following the instructions on the packet. (If there are no instructions, bring a generous amount of water to a boil in a large pan. Add the noodles, and cook for 2 to 3 minutes, testing for doneness.) Drain well, and transfer to serving bowls. Pour on the Soup, and sprinkle with black pepper.

Thai-Style Ramen with Pork and Crispy Wontons

Chinese dried noodles and deep-fried wonton skins go so well with the fish-sauce-flavored soup in this very addictive bowl of noodles.

Serves 2

4 bunches spinach or mustard greens
1 leek, white part only
6 wonton wrappers
Oil for deep frying
7 oz (200 g) dried Chinese wheat noodles (2 packets)
5 oz (150 g) roast pork **(see photo A)**

Soup

2½ cups (600 ml) dashi stock **(see Page 9)**
½ red Thai chili or serrano pepper, deseeded and chopped
¼ cup (45 ml) rice wine or sake
1 tablespoon rice vinegar
2½ tablespoons fish sauce

1 Cut the spinach or greens into 2 inch (5 cm) long pieces. Slice the leek thinly on the diagonal.

2 Put the Soup ingredients and leek in a pan over medium heat. Bring to a boil while skimming off the top. Turn the heat down to low, add the spinach or greens, cover with a lid and simmer for about 3 minutes.

3 Heat up about ⅓ inch (1 cm) of vegetable oil in a pan to 340°F (170°C). Add the wonton wrappers, and deep fry until golden brown, about 1 minute **(see photo B)**.

4 Cook the noodles following the instructions on the packet. Drain and transfer to serving bowls. Pour the Soup over the noodles. Cut the roast pork into ⅓ inch (1 cm) thick slices, and break up the fried wonton wrappers into easy-to-eat pieces. Top the noodles with the pork and wonton wrappers.

....

NOTE This is a Thai-style ramen that's popular at food stalls in Thailand. A wheat flour noodle called *bami* is used, with sliced roast pork or meatballs as toppings. It's usually served from stalls in small bowls.

A Tie up the pork before roasting, and roast while basting with the juices or a marinade of your choice.

B Fry the wonton wrappers in shallow oil while turning them frequently.

Vietnamese Fried Fish Rice Noodle Soup Bun Ca

This soup is very rich because of the deep-fried fish, making the bun (thin rice noodles) so delicious.

Serves 2

½ pound (240 g) boneless whitefish
   filets such as Spanish mackerel,
   sea bass or sea bream
½ clove garlic, peeled and minced
½-inch piece of ginger, peeled and grated
1 teaspoon fish sauce
3 tablespoons flour
Vegetable oil, for deep frying
1 tablespoon sesame oil
6 oz (175 g) dried thin rice noodles

3 leaves romaine lettuce, shredded
4 sprigs fresh dill, roughly chopped
Red pepper powder, to taste

Soup

1⅔ cups (400 ml) dashi stock
   (see Page 9)
½ clove garlic, peeled and minced
½-inch piece of ginger, peeled and grated
3 tablespoons rice wine or sake
2½ tablespoons fish sauce

1 Cut up the fish into bite-sized pieces. Coat with ½ grated garlic clove, ½ grated ginger and 1 teaspoon fish sauce and rub them in well. Dust with the flour.
2 Put the vegetable oil in a pan and add the sesame oil. Heat to 340°F (170°C), and fry the fish until golden brown.
3 Put the Soup ingredients in another pan over medium heat, and bring to a boil.
4 Cook the noodles following the instructions on the packet. Drain and transfer to serving bowls. Pour in the Soup, top with the romaine lettuce and dill, and sprinkle with red pepper powder.

NOTE This rice noodle dish is from Da Nang in central Vietnam. I've added freshness with dill and a spicy kick with red pepper powder.

Vietnamese Chicken Glass Noodle Soup Mien Ga

This simple bowl of glass or cellophane noodles dressed up with chicken broth is so easy on your stomach that I recommend trying it even if you don't have an appetite.

Serves 2

1 large boneless chicken breast, about 7 oz (200 g) total

2 fresh shiitake mushrooms

½ onion

2 deep-fried Japanese or Thai fish cakes

3 tablespoons rice wine or sake

1⅔ cups (400 ml) water

2 tablespoons fish sauce

6 oz (175 g) dried glass or cellophane noodles

3 green onions, cut into ¾ inch (2 cm) long pieces

1 Optionally remove the skin from the chicken breast, and slice into strips on the diagonal.

2 Cut the stems off the shiitake mushrooms and cut the caps into quarters. Slice the onion thinly lengthwise. Cut the fish cakes into ⅔ inch (1.5 cm) wide pieces.

3 Put the sake, water, mushrooms and onion in a pan over medium heat. Bring to a boil. Turn the heat down to low, add the chicken, cover with a lid and simmer for about 6 minutes. Add the fish sauce, taste and add more if needed.

4 Bring a generous amount of water to a boil in another pan and add the noodles. Cook for about 2 minutes, and drain. Add to the pan with the soup, and bring to a boil. Transfer to serving bowls and top with the green onions.

....

NOTE In Vietnamese *mien* means "glass noodles" and *ga* means "chicken." There are many noodle recipes in Vietnam that use noodles besides *banh pho* and bun, such as glass noodles. The deep-fried fish cakes used in this recipe are prefried ones that are readily available in the refrigerated or frozen section of Asian grocery stores.

**Chilled Soba Noodle Soup with
Shrimp Tempura**

Chilled Soba with Okra and Mountain Yam

Chilled Soba Noodle Soup with Shrimp Tempura

These refined deep-fried shrimp are best eaten freshly made. You can use daikon radish or broccoli sprouts as a topping, but any type of sprouts will do.

Serves 2

1¼ cups (300 ml) dashi stock **(see Page 9)**
1 tablespoon rice wine or sake
2 tablespoons soy sauce
Pinch of salt
½ pound (225 g) peeled and deveined small to medium shrimp
Cornstarch for dusting shrimp
4 tablespoons flour
⅔ cup (150 ml) ice water
10 oz (300 g) fresh soba noodles or 7 oz (200 g) dried soba noodles
¼ cup (25 g) bean sprouts

1 Put the dashi stock, rice wine or sake, soy sauce and a pinch of salt in a small pan, and heat over medium. Bring to a boil. Take off the heat and leave to cool to room temperature. Chill in the refrigerator.
2 Sprinkle shrimp with cornstarch and rub it in well. Rinse the starch off (this cleans the shrimp). Pat the shrimp dry with paper towels, and dust with 2 tablespoons of flour.
3 Mix 2 tablespoons of flour with the ice water in a bowl. Do not overmix. Add the shrimp and mix quickly.
4 Heat up some frying oil to 340°F (170°C). Add the shrimp and deep fry until lightly browned.
5 Cook the fresh or dried soba noodles, following the instructions on the packet. Drain well, then rinse in cold running water until completely cool and firm. Drain again. Transfer to serving bowls, pour the chilled soup over them, and top with the shrimp. Trim the ends off the sprouts and put on top of the noodles.

Chilled Soba with Okra and Mountain Yam

This is a very refreshing chilled noodle that's a good choice even on a hot day. *Nagaimo*, or mountain yam, is a long root vegetable that is very sticky and starchy when grated raw. It's available at Chinese, Korean or Japanese grocery stores.

Serves 2

1¼ cups (300 ml) dashi stock **(see Page 9)**
1 tablespoon rice wine or sake
2 tablespoons soy sauce
Pinch of salt
½ pound (225 g) *nagaimo* (Chinese yam or mountain yam) or regular yam or white potatoes
1 lime
4 okra
10 oz (300 g) fresh soba noodles or 7 oz (200 g) dried soba noodles

1 Put the dashi stock, rice wine or sake, soy sauce and a pinch of salt in a small pan, and heat over medium. Bring to a boil. Take off the heat and leave to cool to room temperature. Chill in the refrigerator.
2 Peel and slice the *nagaimo* into thin matchsticks. Slice the limes into thin rounds.
3 Take the calyxes off 4 okra. Sprinkle with a little salt and roll the okra firmly back and forth on a cutting board until the small hairs on the surface are rubbed off. Rinse the okra. Bring a small pan of water to a boil, and blanch the okra for 30 seconds. Drain, refresh in ice water, and drain again. Cut in half lengthwise.
4 Cook the fresh or dried soba noodles, following the instructions on the packet. Drain well, then rinse in cold running water until completely cool and firm. Drain again. Transfer to serving bowls, pour the chilled soup over them, and top with the *nagaimo* yam, okra and lime.

NOTE Hot and sour soup is representative of the cuisine of Sichuan Province in China. Here I have made it into a noodle soup. The hot-and-sour soup I had on my travels had a perfect balance between its various flavors, and the black pepper added at the end was especially memorable.

A The vinegar, which is indispensable in a hot and sour soup, is added after pork and vegetables are stir fried, with the sake and water.

B Scoop up easy-to-eat pieces of tofu with a spoon, and add at the end of the cooking process.

Hot and Sour Noodle Soup

Packed with the flavors of pork, bamboo shoots and dried scallops, this soup is absolutely delicious. The black pepper added at the end is essential to make this dish sing.

Serves 2

3 dried scallops
4 oz (120 g) thinly sliced pork loin
$2/3$ cup (80g) precooked bamboo shoots, vacuum packed or canned
Small bunch enoki mushrooms
2 teaspoons sesame oil
1-inch piece of ginger, peeled and grated

Soup
2 tablespoons rice wine or sake
2 tablespoons rice vinegar
$1^2/3$ cups (400 ml) water

Flavorings
2 teaspoons sesame chili oil
2 tablespoons soy sauce
$1/4$ teaspoon salt

5 oz (150 g) firm tofu
7 oz (200 g) dried thin wheat noodles
Freshly grated black pepper to taste

1 Soak the dried scallops (available at Chinese grocery stores) in water to cover overnight until softened. Shred, and reserve the soaking liquid.
2 Slice the pork and bamboo shoots into thin strips. Remove the root ends from the enoki mushrooms and cut into 1 inch (3 cm) long pieces.
3 Place a pan over medium heat and add the sesame oil and ginger. When the oil is fragrant, add the pork, bamboo shoots and enoki mushrooms, and stir fry until the pork changes color.
4 Add the shredded scallops with the soaking liquid to the pan. Add the Soup ingredients **(see photo A)**, and bring to a boil while skimming the surface.
5 Turn the heat down to low, cover with a lid and simmer for 10 minutes. Add the Flavorings. Spoon off pieces of the tofu and put into the pan **(see photo B)**, and bring back to a boil.
6 Cook the noodles following the instructions on the packet. Drain well and put into serving bowls. Add the Soup, and sprinkle with black pepper.

NOTE There are many small bowls of noodle soups on offer at diners and food stalls in Taiwan, and these *ta-a* noodles are one of them. Containing ground pork and cilantro, it's one of Taiwan's most famous dishes. It looks very simple, but the delicious flavors stay with you for a long time.

A Hard-boiled eggs marinated in a sweet-salty sauce are indispensable to *ta-a* noodles.

B After adding the flavoring ingredients and the dried and soaked ingredients, stir fry to the point where there is still some moisture left in the pan before adding the soaking liquids.

Minced Pork Noodle Soup   Ta-a or Danzi Noodles

The umami-rich dried shiitake mushrooms, dried shrimp and ground pork blend well with the soup to create a rich flavor that matches well with the plump noodles.

Serves 2

2 dried shiitake mushrooms
¼ cup (25 g) dried shrimp
1 teaspoon sesame oil
1-inch piece of ginger, peeled and minced
4 oz (120 g) ground pork
7 oz (200 g) dried thin wheat noodles
2 marinated hard-boiled eggs *(see photo A and Page 9)*, cut in half
4 sprigs fresh cilantro (coriander leaves)

Flavorings
3 tablespoons Shaoxing wine or sake
2 tablespoons soy sauce

1 Soak the dried shiitake mushrooms in 2 cups plus 2 tablespoons (500 ml) water overnight to reconstitute them. Soak the dried shrimp in enough lukewarm water to cover for about 20 minutes. Chop both up roughly (remove the hard stem ends of the shiitake mushrooms first). Reserve the soaking liquid of each.

2 Heat up a pan over medium and add the sesame oil and ginger. When the oil is fragrant, add the ground pork and stir fry until the meat changes color.

3 Add the Flavorings, shiitake mushrooms and shrimp to the pan and stir fry for about a minute *(see photo B)*. Add the soaking liquid from the mushrooms and shrimp, and bring to a boil while skimming the surface. Turn the heat down to low, cover with a lid and simmer for about 8 minutes.

4 Cook the noodles following the instructions on the packet. Drain well, and transfer to serving bowls. Pour in the soup and top with the eggs and cilantro.

Fish Ball and Celery Noodle Soup

This is a very light noodle soup with a fish-based broth. The celery leaves added at the end impart a wonderful aroma.

Serves 2

7 oz (200 g) whitefish such as Spanish mackerel, sea bass or sea bream

½ stalk celery

4 celery leaves

1 leek, white part only

8 oz (240 g) fresh Chinese lo mein noodles

1 tablespoon fish sauce

Fish Ball Mixture

½ cup (50 g) semi-dried or dried whitebait

1-inch piece of ginger, peeled and minced

1 egg white

½ teaspoon salt

1 tablespoon rice wine or sake

2 teaspoons sesame oil

Soup

1⅔ cups (400 ml) dashi stock (see Page 9)

3 tablespoons rice wine or sake

1 Remove skin and bones from the fish and cut into 3 to 4 pieces. Put the pieces in a food processor with the Fish Ball Mixture ingredients. Process until smooth.

2 Remove the strings from the celery and cut into ¼ inch (6 mm) thick slices. Finely chop the leek.

3 Put the Soup ingredients and the celery and leek into a pan over medium heat. When it comes to a boil, divide the Fish Ball Mixture into 4 portions, form into balls and drop into the soup. Bring back to a boil, turn the heat down to low, cover with a lid and simmer for about 6 minutes. Slice the celery leaves thinly, and add to the Soup along with the fish sauce.

4 Cook the noodles following the instructions on the packet. (If there are no instructions, bring a generous amount of water to a boil in a large pan. Add the noodles, and cook for 2 to 3 minutes, testing for doneness.) Drain well, and transfer to serving bowls. Pour the Soup and fish balls into the bowls.

....

NOTE I've taken a fish ball soup recipe and turned it into a noodle soup. By using dried whitebait as well as whitefish, the fish balls will have a deeper more complex flavor.

Ramen with Beef and Tomato Soup

The beef-flavored soup combined with the tanginess of the tomatoes makes for a memorable flavor!

Serves 2

8 oz (230 g) fresh Chinese lo mein noodles
4 oz (120 g) thinly sliced beef
2 medium tomatoes
1 bunch bok choi
1 tablespoon soy sauce
2 teaspoons fish sauce

Soup

$1\frac{2}{3}$ cups (400 ml) dashi stock **(see Page 9)**
1 clove garlic, peeled and crushed
$\frac{1}{4}$ cup (45 ml) rice wine or sake

1 Cut the tomatoes into 6 wedges each. Cut the bok choi into 6 wedges and remove the root ends.
2 Put the Soup ingredients in a pan over medium heat. When it comes to a boil, add the tomatoes. Add the beef one slice at a time, and skim off any fat.
3 Add the soy sauce and the fish sauce along with the bok choi. Bring the Soup back to a boil and add the sesame oil.
4 Cook the noodles following the instructions on the packet. (If there are no instructions, bring a generous amount of water to a boil in a large pan. Add the noodles, and cook for 2 to 3 minutes, testing for doneness.) Drain well, and transfer to serving bowls. Pour the Soup over the noodles.

NOTE The fat and flavor from the beef add a welcome heartiness and heft to offset the lightness of the noodles and broth.

Fresh Clam Noodle Soup

Raw *shijimi* clams marinated in a soy-based sauce give this dish a fresh, clean, oceany taste. Here I have used the umami of *shijimi* clams in a very nutritious and flavorful noodle soup.

Serves 2

7 oz (200 g) fresh *shijimi* clams or small littleneck clams, in shells, cleaned and soaked in salted water to remove the grit

2 teaspoons sesame oil

6 stalks watercress, cut into 2 inch (5 cm) long pieces

7 oz (200 g) thin dried wheat noodles

Soup

1 clove garlic, peeled and thinly sliced

1-inch piece of unpeeled ginger, thinly sliced

3 tablespoons rice wine or sake

1½ tablespoons fish sauce

2 cups plus 2 tablespoons (500 ml) water

1 Put the Soup ingredients in a pan over medium heat. When it comes to a boil, add the well-cleaned clams. Bring back to a boil while skimming off the surface.

2 Turn the heat down to low, cover with a lid and simmer for about 8 minutes. Turn off the heat and add the sesame oil and watercress.

3 Cook the noodles following the instructions on the packet. Drain well and transfer to serving bowls. Pour the Soup over the noodles.

Glass Noodle Soup with Bamboo Shoots

This subtle soup has a refined, gentle flavor that soothes. The crunchy texture of the fresh woodear mushrooms adds a great accent.

Serves 2

¼ cup (25 g) dried shrimp

½ cup (75 g) precooked bamboo shoots, vacuum packed or canned

3 large fresh woodear mushrooms

5 oz (120 g) dried rice vermicelli

3 thin green onions, chopped

Soup

2½ cups (600 ml) dashi stock **(see Page 9)**

1-inch piece of ginger, peeled and shredded

2 tablespoons rice wine or sake

1 tablespoon soy sauce

Flavorings

¼ teaspoon salt

2 teaspoons sesame oil

1 Put the dried shrimp in a bowl and add enough lukewarm water to cover. Leave to soak and soften for about 20 minutes, and chop roughly. Reserve the soaking liquid.

2 Slice the bamboo shoots into thin matchsticks. Cut the stems off the woodear mushrooms and chop up into easy-to-eat pieces.

3 Put the Soup ingredients, the reconstituted dried shrimp and its soaking liquid in a pan over medium heat. When it comes to a boil add the bamboo shoots and woodear mushrooms, and bring to a boil again while skimming the foam. Turn the heat down to low, cover with a lid and simmer for about 6 minutes. Add the Flavorings.

4 Cook the noodles following the instructions on the packet. Drain well and transfer to serving bowls. Pour the Soup over the noodles, and scatter with the green onions.

NOTE This noodle soup made with beef or pork intestines and thin wheat noodles that thicken the soup is very popular at food stalls at the night markets in Taiwan. The noodles are usually quite short and scooped up with a spoon to eat. In Taiwan, a very thin wheat noodle called *mee sua* is used. Here I have used somen noodles, but use whichever one you want or can find.

A Parboil the beef intestines to get rid of their distinct gamy odor and make them easier to eat.

B By adding the noodles without boiling them first, the soup is thickened.

Vermicelli Soup with Tripe

This very flavorful rice soup contains beef intestines and oyster sauce. The thin noodles are added without boiling them first, imparting a distinctive creamy texture to the soup and making it even tastier.

Serves 2

7 oz (200 g) beef tripe or small intestines
5 oz (150 g) dried very thin wheat noodles such as somen
6 sprigs fresh cilantro (coriander leaves)
Coarsely ground red chili pepper, to taste

Soup
2½ cups (600 ml) dashi stock **(see Page 9)**
1-inch piece of ginger, peeled and shredded
3 tablespoons rice wine or sake
2 tablespoons oyster sauce
1 tablespoon rice vinegar

Flavorings
1 tablespoon soy sauce
2 teaspoons sesame oil

1 Boil the beef intestines for 2 minutes **(see photo A)**, drain and rinse well under cold running water. Cut into bite-sized pieces.
2 Put the Soup ingredients in a pan over medium heat. When it comes to a boil, add the beef intestines, and bring back to a boil while skimming the surface.
3 Turn the heat down to low, cover with a lid and simmer for about 8 minutes. Add the Flavorings and the noodles **(see photo B)**, and simmer until the Soup is thickened, about 2½ minutes.
4 Transfer to serving bowls, scatter on the cilantro/coriander, and sprinkle with the coarsely ground red chili pepper.

SOMEN NOODLES
Somen are very thin wheat noodles that are usually served chilled. I've used them in this recipe instead of Taiwanese *mee sua*.

Korean Cold Noodles Mul Naengmyeon

The springy, chewy texture of the *naengmyeon* noodles matches well with the subtly sour, chilled soup.

Serves 2

4 oz (120 g) boiled pork (see Page 13)
4-inch (10-cm) piece daikon radish
½ large cucumber
⅓ teaspoon salt
½ medium tomato
¼ medium apple
7 oz (200 g) dried *naengmyeon* noodles
⅓ cup (50 g) chopped cabbage kimchi
2 teaspoons toasted white sesame seeds

Soup

1⅔ cups (400 ml) dried sardine dashi
    stock (see Page 81)
1½ tablespoons fish sauce
1 tablespoon black vinegar

1 Combine the Soup ingredients, and chill in the refrigerator.
2 Cut the daikon radish in half lengthwise and slice into thin half-rounds. Cut the cucumber in half lengthwise, remove the seeds, and slice thinly on the diagonal. Sprinkle the daikon radish and cucumber with ⅙ teaspoon each of salt (divide ⅓ teaspoon of salt in half), rubbing it in. When the pieces have turned limp, squeeze tightly to remove any excess moisture.
3 Cut the tomato in half and slice into ¼ inch (6 mm) thick half-rounds. Slice the unpeeled apple lengthwise into thin slices.
4 Cook the noodles following the instructions on the packet. Drain into a colander, and rinse well under cold running water until completely cooled and firm in texture. Drain again, transfer to serving bowls, and pour the chilled Soup over them. Slice the pork and place on the noodles along with the vegetables, apple and kimchi. Sprinkle with the sesame seeds.

NOTE There are two types of chilled noodles, or *naengmyeon*, in Korea. One is called *bibim naengmyeon*, a spicy mixed noodle dish without soup, and the other is *mul naengmyeon* (*mul* means "water"), this recipe.

Korean Beef Short Ribs with Glass Noodles   Yukhoe Jiang Dangmyeon

The rich, spicy gochujang-flavored soup is toned down by the mild creaminess of the poached egg.

Serves 2

- 4 oz (120 g) dried glass or cellophane noodles
- 5 oz (150 g) boneless beef short ribs
- 2 teaspoons sesame oil
- 1 clove garlic, peeled and thinly sliced
- 1-inch piece of unpeeled ginger, thinly sliced
- 1⅔ cups (400 ml) dried sardine dashi stock **(see Page 81)**
- 3 tablespoons Shaoxing wine or sake
- 1½ teaspoons gochujang (Korean red chili paste)
- 1 tablespoon soy sauce
- 2 eggs
- 2 teaspoons rice vinegar
- ¾ cup (125 g) soybean sprouts, thin roots cut off
- 3 thin green onions, sliced into ¾ inch (2 cm) long diagonal pieces

1 Put the glass noodles in a large bowl or pan and add enough boiling water to cover. Leave to soak for about 10 minutes until softened, then drain. Cut the beef into ⅓ inch (1 cm) wide pieces.

2 Place a pan over medium heat and add the sesame oil, garlic and ginger. When the oil is fragrant, add the beef, and stir fry until the meat changes color. Remove the beef from the pan.

3 Add the dried sardine stock and Shaoxing wine or sake and bring to a boil over medium heat. Add the drained noodles, gochujang and soy sauce, and turn the heat down to low. Cover with a lid and simmer for about 5 minutes.

4 Add a generous amount of water and the vinegar to another small pan and heat over medium heat. Break in the eggs and make soft-set poached eggs.

5 Put the soup and noodles in bowls. Top with the beef, poached eggs, bean sprouts and green onions.

....

NOTE I added glass noodles to *yukhoe jiang,* a spicy soup with beef and bean sprouts. If you swap the noodles with rice this becomes *yukhoe jiang gukbap.*

Japanese Soba with Fish Cake and Egg

Kayaku soba is a type of soba noodle soup with *yaku*, or medicinal herbs, on top. For me, this is a very comforting, nostalgic dish. Slice the fish cake thinly so that it can absorb the flavors of the soup well.

Serves 2

½ Japanese fish cake (2 oz or 60 g)
5 sprigs *mitsuba* or watercress
1⅔ cups (400ml) dashi stock **(see Page 9)**
1 tablespoon rice wine or sake
1 tablespoon mirin or sherry
Pinch of salt
2 tablespoons soy sauce
2 eggs
10 oz (300 g) fresh soba noodles or
    7 oz (200 g) dried soba noodles

1 Slice the fish cake thinly. Roughly chop up the *mitsuba* or watercress sprigs.
2 Put the dashi stock, rice wine or sake, mirin or sherry, a pinch of salt and the sliced fish cake into a small pan, and heat over medium. Bring to a boil and add the soy sauce.
3 Beat the eggs and swirl them into the pan. Just before it comes back to a boil, turn off the heat.
4 Cook the fresh or dried soba noodles, following the instructions on the packet. Drain well, then rinse in cold running water until completely cool and firm. Drain again, then reheat by putting the noodles in a pan of boiling water for a few seconds. Drain once more and put into serving bowls. Add the soup and fish cake, and top with the *mitsuba* or watercress.

Chicken Soup Soba

Chicken *nanban* is a regional speciality of Miyazaki Prefecture that's popular throughout Japan. This soba version tastes lighter if you remove the skin from the chicken. Or leave the skin on for a more succulent, decadent version.

Serves 2

2 boneless chicken thighs, about 7 oz (200 g)
1 leek, white part only
1⅔ cups (400ml) dashi stock **(see Page 9)**
1 tablespoon rice wine or sake
1 tablespoon mirin or sherry
Pinch of salt
2 tablespoons soy sauce
10 oz (300 g) fresh soba noodles or 7 oz
    (200 g) dried soba noodles
Shichimi togarashi (seven-flavor chili
    powder), to taste

1 Optionally remove the skin from the chicken thighs. Cut the chicken into bite-sized pieces. Cut the leek into 2 inch (5 cm) long pieces, then cut each piece into half lengthwise.
2 Put the dashi stock, rice wine or sake, mirin or sherry and a pinch of salt into a pan, and heat over medium. Bring to a boil and add the chicken.
3 When the pan comes back to a boil, skim off any foam, turn the heat down to low and add the soy sauce. Simmer for about 7 minutes.
4 Cook the fresh or dried soba noodles, following the instructions on the packet. Drain well, then rinse in cold running water until completely cool and firm. Drain again, then reheat by putting the noodles in a pan of boiling water for a few seconds. Drain once more and put into serving bowls. Pour the soup on top, add the chicken and sprinkle on some *shichimi togarashi* (seven-flavor chili pepper powder).

Japanese Soba with Fish Cake and Egg

Chicken Soup Soba

Knife-Cut Noodles Kal-Guksu

In Korean *kal* means "knife," and *guksu* means "noodle." This noodle soup is made with thick handmade wheat noodles that resemble udon. Here I've used dried udon noodles to save time and effort.

Serves 2

7 oz (200g) dried udon noodles or similar thick wheat noodles
7 oz (200g) fresh littleneck clams, in shells, cleaned and soaked in salted water to remove the grit
½ zucchini
½ yellow squash
2 sheets nori seaweed, well-shredded
2 teaspoons toasted white sesame seeds

Soup

1-inch piece of unpeeled ginger, sliced thinly
2 tablespoons rice wine or sake
1½ tablespoons fish sauce
2 cups plus 2 tablespoons (500 ml) water

1 Wash the clams very well. Slice the zucchini and squash into thin rounds.
2 Put the Soup ingredients in a pan over medium heat. When it comes to a boil, add the clams and vegetables, and bring back to a boil while skimming the surface. Turn the heat down to low, cover with a lid and simmer for about 5 minutes. Add the seaweed and simmer briefly.
3 Cook the noodles following the instructions on the packet. Drain well, and transfer to serving bowls. Pour in the Soup, and sprinkle with sesame seeds.

Spicy Pork Belly Noodles

This noodle soup is reminiscent of *gamjatang*, a spicy Korean stew made with pork. The potatoes are cooked until they melt into the noodles.

Serves 2

5 oz (150 g) pork belly
2 medium potatoes
1 bunch spinach
1 teaspoon sesame oil
7 oz (200 g) dried Chinese wheat noodles
2 teaspoons ground black sesame seeds (available at Korean or Japanese grocery stores, or grind up whole sesame seeds with a mortar and pestle)

Soup

1 clove garlic, peeled and crushed
1 teaspoon gochujang (Korean red chili paste)
¼ cup (45 ml) Shaoxing wine or sake
¼ teaspoon salt
2½ cups (600 ml) water

1 Cut the pork into 1½ inch (4 cm) wide pieces. Peel and quarter the potatoes. Cut up the spinach into easy-to-eat pieces.
2 Heat up the sesame oil in a pan over medium. Add the pork and stir fry until the meat changes color.
3 Add the Soup ingredients and the potatoes to the pan, and bring to a boil while skimming off the surface. Turn the heat down to low, cover with a lid and simmer for about 12 minutes. Add the spinach and simmer briefly.
4 Cook the noodles following the instructions on the packet. Drain well, and transfer to serving bowls. Pour in the Soup, and sprinkle with the black sesame seeds.

NOTE *Kongguksu* is a chilled noodle soup from Korea. It is made with a soybean-paste-based soup and thin wheat noodles. When I had it in South Korea, it was so memorable that I have recreated it here. Cucumber and kimchi are the usual toppings, but here I have used salted turnips instead.

A Soak dried sardines or other dried whitebait and *kombu* seaweed in water overnight, then heat through to make the dashi stock.

B Add the dried sardine dashi stock to the boiled soybeans, and process in a mixer until smooth.

Cold Korean Noodles in Soy Milk Kongguksu

Homemade soy milk is so delicious, it's a revelation! This highly nutritious noodle soup is easy to eat even on a hot day when you have little appetite.

Serves 2

½ cup (100 g) dried soybeans
1⅔ cups (400 ml) dried sardine stock
   (see recipe below)
2 tablespoons fish sauce
2 small white turnips with greens
⅓ teaspoon salt
7 oz (200 g) thin dried wheat noodles
Coarsely grated red chili pepper to taste

**How to Make Niboshi Dashi
(Dried Sardine Stock)**
Makes 4½ cups (1 l): Remove the guts and heads from 7 dried sardines, and split into half lengthwise. Put 4½ cups (1 l) of water and a 2-inch (5-cm) square piece of dried *kombu* seaweed in a bowl with the sardines, and refrigerate overnight. Transfer the contents of the bowl to a pan over medium heat and bring to a boil **(see photo A)**. Take out the sardines and *kombu* seaweed. The stock can be kept in the refrigerator for up to 2 days.

1 Soak the soybeans in cold water to cover overnight.
2 Drain the soaked soybeans, put into a pan and add enough water to cover over medium heat. Bring to a boil while skimming the surface.
3 Lower the heat to medium-low, and cook the beans until you can smash one easily between your finger and thumb, about 50 minutes. Keep adding hot water to ensure the beans are always covered.
4 Drain the cooked soybeans and put into a mixer. Add the dried sardine stock and process **(see photo B)**. Mix in the fish sauce and chill in the refrigerator.
5 Cut the turnips into about 10 wedges each. Sprinkle with half the salt and leave for 10 minutes. When the turnips are limp, squeeze them very tightly to eliminate excess moisture. Cut the turnip greens into ⅓ inch (1 cm) long pieces, sprinkle with the remaining salt, rub it in well and then squeeze to eliminate excess moisture.
6 Cook the noodles following the instructions on the packet. Drain, then rinse under cold running water until completely cooled and firm. Drain well and transfer to serving bowls. Pour the chilled soup into the bowls and add a few ice cubes. Top with the turnip and turnip greens, and sprinkle on some chili pepper.

Spicy Sichuan Dan Dan Noodles

The key to making a flavorful, rich soup is the double use of sesame seeds.

Serves 2

½ onion
1 bunch bok choi
8 oz (230 g) fresh Chinese lo mein noodles
2 teaspoons sesame oil
1 clove garlic, peeled and minced
1-inch piece of ginger, peeled and finely
  chopped
½ teaspoon spicy Sichuan bean paste
  (*doubanjiang*)
5 oz (150 g) ground pork
4 tablespoons Chinese or Japanese sesame
  paste, or tahini
1 tablespoon toasted whole sesame seeds
1 tablespoon soy sauce
½ teaspoon salt
Spicy chili sesame oil, to taste
Ground white sesame seeds to taste

Soup

3 tablespoons Shaoxing wine or sake
1⅔ cups (400 ml) water

1 Slice the onion thinly lengthwise. Slice the stems of the bok choi into thin diagonal pieces, and roughly chop up the leaves.

2 Heat up a pan over medium heat and add the sesame oil, garlic, ginger and *doubanjiang*. When the oil is fragrant, add the pork, and stir fry until the meat changes color. Add the Soup ingredients and bring to a boil while skimming off the surface.

3 Add the sesame paste and sesame seeds and mix to blend. Add the bok choi, turn the heat down to low and simmer for about 2 minutes. Add the soy sauce and salt.

4 Cook the noodles following the instructions on the packet. (If there are no instructions, bring a generous amount of water to a boil in a large pan. Add the noodles, and cook for 2 to 3 minutes, testing for doneness.) Drain well, and transfer to serving bowls. Pour the Soup into the bowls, and add chili sesame oil and ground sesame seeds to taste.

NOTE These spicy noodles with stir-fried pork from Sichuan Province in China have grown in popularity as the region's fiery culinary offerings have.

Pork and Vegetable Noodles

Packed with pork and vegetables, this noodle soup has a deep yet light flavor.
The thickened broth coats the noodles nicely.

Serves 2

5 oz (150 g) thinly sliced pork
3 tablespoons cornstarch
2 napa cabbage leaves
½ carrot
2 baby corn
2 teaspoons sesame oil
8 snow peas
1 tablespoon soy sauce
½ teaspoon salt
8 oz (240 g) fresh Chinese lo mein noodles
Freshly ground black pepper to taste

Soup

1⅔ cups (400 ml) dashi stock **(see Page 9)**
3 tablespoons rice wine or sake

1 Cut the pork into 1 inch (3 cm) wide pieces, and dust with the cornstarch.
2 Slice the stems of the napa cabbage into thin diagonal pieces, and roughly cut up the leaves. Cut the carrot into matchsticks. Slice the baby corn in half lengthwise.
3 Heat the sesame oil in a pan over medium. Add the pork and stir fry until the meat changes color. Add the napa cabbage, carrot and baby corn and stir fry until limp. Add the Soup ingredients and bring to a boil. Turn the heat down to low, cover with a lid and simmer for about 5 minutes.
4 Remove the strings from the snow peas and add them with the soy sauce and salt to the pan. Simmer until the soup is slightly thickened.
5 Cook the noodles following the instructions on the packet. (If there are no instructions, bring a generous amount of water to a boil. Add the noodles, and cook for 2 to 3 minutes, testing for doneness.) Drain well, and transfer to serving bowls. Pour the Soup into the bowls, and sprinkle with black pepper to taste.

NOTE This ingredient-packed bowl of noodles with a thickened broth offers diners a little bit of everything. Try adding shrimp or boiled quail eggs for an even more complex concoction.

Serves 2

8 oz (240 g) firm tofu
1 tablespoon sesame oil
1 clove garlic, peeled and finely chopped
1-inch piece of ginger, peeled and finely
  chopped
½ teaspoon spicy Sichuan bean paste
  (*doubanjiang*)
4 oz (120 g) ground pork
1 teaspoon coarsely ground Sichuan
  peppercorn or black pepper
1 leek, white part only
1 tablespoon cornstarch
8 oz (240 g) fresh Chinese lo mein noodles

Soup
2½ cups (600 ml) dashi stock **(see Page 9)**
1 tablespoon rice wine or sake
1½ tablespoons soy sauce
¼ teaspoon salt

Sichuan-Style Pork and Tofu Noodles Ma Po Mian

The zing and fragrance of the Sichuan peppercorn (*hua jiao*) brings the flavors together. Mix the noodles, the thick *ma po* sauce and tofu together well!

1 Put a weight such as a cutting board with a bowl of water on top on the tofu, and leave for about an hour to drain off the excess water. Cut into ⅔ inch (1.5 cm) cubes.
2 Heat up a frying pan over medium and add ½ tablespoon of sesame oil, the garlic, ginger and *doubanjiang*. When the oil is fragrant, add the ground pork, and stir fry until the meat changes color.
3 Add ⅓ of the combined Soup ingredients to the frying pan, and bring to a boil while skimming the surface. Turn the heat down to low, cover with a lid and simmer for about 5 minutes.
4 Add the Sichuan peppercorn and leek to the frying pan. Dissolve the cornstarch in 2 tablespoons of water, and stir into the soup to thicken it. Bring to a boil, and add the rest of the sesame oil.
5 Put the remaining ⅔ of the Soup ingredients in a separate pan, and bring to a boil over medium heat.
6 Cook the noodles following the instructions on the packet. (If there are no instructions, bring a generous amount of water to a boil in a large pan. Add the noodles, and cook for 2 to 3 minutes, testing for doneness.) Drain well, and transfer to serving bowls. Pour the Soup into the bowls, and ladle the pork and tofu mixture on top.

NOTE This dish is based on a classic Chinese noodle soup called *pai gu mian*, or *pa-ko-men* in Japan, made with pork pieces on the bone. A very similar dish is made with beef in Vietnam and chicken in other parts of Southeast Asia. Here I have made a version with boneless chicken thigh pieces.

A Add the five-spice powder and other flavoring ingredients to the chicken and rub it in well.

B The key is to raise the heat the last few seconds to crisp up the surface of the chicken.

Serves 2

4 boneless chicken thighs, about 14 oz (400 g)
Vegetable oil for deep frying
3 tablespoons cornstarch
½ cup (120 g) spinach
1 leek, white part only
8 oz (240 g) fresh Chinese lo mein noodles

Chicken Flavorings
¼ teaspoon five-spice powder
2 tablespoons Shaoxing wine or sake
2 tablespoons soy sauce

Soup
2½ cups (600 ml) dashi stock **(see Page 9)**
¼ teaspoon salt
2 tablespoons Shaoxing wine or sake
2 tablespoons soy sauce

Fried Chicken Soup Noodles

This is a dynamic noodle dish topped with fried chicken. The chicken tastes great both when it's freshly fried and after it's absorbed some of the soup.

1 Optionally remove the skin from the chicken thigh meat. Lightly pound the thicker parts of the meat with the side of a heavy kitchen knife so that it is even in thickness all around. Rub the Chicken Flavorings into the meat **(see photo A)**.
2 Heat up 2 inches (5 cm) of vegetable oil in a frying pan to 320°F (160°C). Coat the chicken pieces in cornstarch, and fry on both sides until golden brown **(see photo B)**. Raise the heat to high for the last few seconds to crisp up the surface of the chicken. Drain off the oil.
3 Put the Soup ingredients in a pan over medium heat and bring to a boil. Add the spinach and chopped leek, and simmer briefly.
4 Cook the noodles following the instructions on the packet. (If there are no instructions, bring a generous amount of water to a boil in a large pan. Add the noodles, and cook for 2 to 3 minutes, testing for doneness.) Drain well, and transfer to serving bowls. Pour the Soup into the bowls. Cut the chicken into easy-to-eat pieces and place on top of the noodles.

A Adjust the amount of water added so that the dough doesn't stick to your hands.

B Cover in plastic wrap to prevent the dough from drying out. If it's frozen, the dough's easier to shave with a peeler.

NOTE: The noodles in this distinctive dish from Shanxi Province in China are shaved off a block of dough directly into the pot. You could use dried flat wheat noodles like *kishimen*, but here I show you how to make your own dough and freeze it before shaving it with a vegetable peeler. I hope you give these delicious homemade noodles a try.

C Peel off long strips of the dough using a vegetable peeler before boiling them.

Chinese Hand-Cut Noodles Dao Xiao Mian

These noodles have such a wonderful slippery-smooth texture because they're homemade! They're an ideal match with the well-flavored ground beef with dried shrimp.

Serves 2

1 tablespoon dried shrimp
¼ cup (40 g) Chinese *zha cai* pickles, pickled mustard greens or sauerkraut
1 tablespoon plus 2 teaspoons sesame oil
1-inch piece of ginger, peeled and finely chopped
10 oz (300 g) *dao xiao mian* noodles **(see sidebar for recipe)**
5 oz (150 g) ground beef
6 sprigs fresh cilantro (coriander leaves)
Spicy sesame chili oil, to taste

Soup

2 tablespoons Shaoxing wine or sake
2½ cups (600 ml) water

1 Soak the dried shrimp in enough lukewarm water to cover for about 30 minutes to soften them. Drain and chop roughly, reserving the soaking liquid. Slice the *zha cai* pickles thinly, and soak in cold water to cover for about 10 minutes to remove some of the salt. Drain and chop roughly.

2 Heat up a skillet over medium. Add 2 teaspoons of sesame oil and the ginger. When the oil is fragrant, add the ground beef and stir fry until the meat changes color.

3 Add the soaked shrimp with the reserved soaking liquid, the *zha cai* pickles and the Soup ingredients to the frying pan. Bring to a boil while skimming the surface. Turn the heat down to low, cover with a lid and simmer for about 5 minutes.

4 Bring some water to a boil in a separate pan and add 1 tablespoon sesame oil. Add the shaved *dao xiao mian* and cook for about 40 seconds. Drain.

5 Transfer the noodles to serving bowls, pour in the Soup, top with the cilantro and add sesame chili oil to taste.

How to Make Dao Xiao Mian Dough

Put ¾ cup (80 g) bread flour, ½ cup (50 g) cake flour, ¼ teaspoon salt and 1 tablespoon sesame oil in a bowl. Add ¼ to ⅓ cup (70 to 80 ml) water little by little while mixing **(see photo A)**. When the dough no longer sticks to your hands, knead on a floured surface and form into an oval shape. Cover with plastic wrap and freeze for about 2 hours **(see photo B)**. Peel off long strips using a vegetable peeler **(see photo C)** before boiling.

Pickled Mustard Greens and Pork Noodles

The key to this dish is the *takanazuke*, pickled mustard greens, found in Asian markets or online. Combined with the pork, it becomes unforgettably delicious.

1 Finely chop the pickled mustard greens. Slice the pork into thin strips.

2 Make a cut into the leek lengthwise, remove the core and shred finely. Put the shreds in a bowl of cold water to crisp. Drain.

3 Heat up a pan over medium. Add the sesame oil and ginger. When the oil is fragrant, add the mustard greens and pork, and stir fry until the meat changes color.

4 Add the black vinegar and stir fry briefly. Add the Soup ingredients and bring to a boil while skimming the surface. Turn the heat down to low, cover with a lid and simmer for about 5 minutes.

5 Cook the noodles following the instructions on the packet. (If there are no instruction, bring a generous amount of water to a boil in a large pan. Add the noodles, and cook for 2 to 3 minutes, testing for doneness.) Drain well, and transfer to serving bowls. Pour the Soup into the bowls, and top with the shredded leek.

Serves 2

½ cup (80 g) pickled mustard greens

4 oz (120 g) thinly sliced pork

1 leek, white part only

2 teaspoons sesame oil

1-inch piece of ginger, peeled and finely chopped

1 tablespoon black vinegar

8 oz (240 g) fresh Chinese lo mein noodles

Soup

2½ cups (600ml) dashi stock **(see Page 9)**

1 tablespoon rice wine or sake

¼ teaspoon salt

1½ tablespoons soy sauce

Shrimp Wonton Noodles

The shrimp-stuffed, umami-packed wontons match well with the simple dashi stock.

1 Peel and devein the shrimp. Sprinkle with the cornstarch, and rub it in well. Rinse under running water (this cleans the shrimp). Pat dry with paper towels. Chop up roughly, and mix well with the ginger, salt and sake.

2 Put 1 teaspoon of the shrimp mixture in the center of a wonton wrapper. Wet the edge of the wrapper and fold into a triangle. Repeat with the rest of the shrimp and wrappers. Bring a pan of water to a boil and cook the wontons for 2 minutes.

3 Put the Soup ingredients in another pan over medium heat. When it comes to a boil, add the wontons and baby bok choi, turn the heat down to low, and simmer for about 2 minutes.

4 Cook the noodles following the instructions on the packet. Drain well and transfer to serving bowls. Pour the Soup over the noodles, and sprinkle with the red chili pepper flakes.

Serves 2

8 medium shrimp, about 4 oz (120 g) total
2 tablespoons cornstarch
1-inch piece of ginger, finely chopped
$\frac{1}{4}$ teaspoon salt
2 teaspoons rice wine or sake
8 to 10 wonton wrappers
2 baby bok choi
7 oz (200 g) dried shrimp roe noodles
Red chili pepper flakes to taste

Soup

$2\frac{1}{2}$ cups (600 ml) dashi stock **(see Page 9)**
1 tablespoon rice wine or sake
$1\frac{1}{2}$ tablespoons soy sauce
$\frac{1}{4}$ teaspoon salt

Roast Pork and Pea Shoot Noodles
Char Siu Ramen

Char siu ramen is a standard type of ramen noodle soup, made with a simple soy-sauce-flavored broth. The *char siu* (roast pork) is usually sliced thin, but here I've cut it into thick meaty chunks.

1 Cut the roast pork into 1 inch (3cm) thick cubes. Trim the ends off the pea shoots, and cut into 1 inch (3cm) long pieces.

2 Put the Soup ingredients in a pan over medium heat. When it comes to a boil, add the roast pork, turn the heat down to low, cover with a lid and simmer for about 5 minutes. Add the pea shoots and simmer briefly.

3 Cook the fresh Chinese noodles following the instructions on the packet. (If there are no instructions, bring a generous amount of water to a boil in a large pan. Add the noodles, and cook for about 2 minutes, testing for doneness.) Drain and transfer to serving bowls. Pour the Soup over the noodles.

Serves 2

7 oz (200 g) roast pork
½ cup (45 g) pea shoots
8 oz (240 g) fresh Chinese thin lo mein egg noodles

Soup
2½ cups (600 ml) dashi stock **(see Page 9)**
1 tablespoon rice wine or sake
1½ tablespoons soy sauce
¼ teaspoon salt

Sweet Endings

After enjoying noodles from around Asia, end your meal with a dessert from the region. Here I show you how to make some sweet treats from Vietnam, Taiwan and China.

Mango Pudding

This pudding, made with fresh mangoes, is a summertime favorite. Enhance the natural sweetness of the fruit with cinnamon.

Makes 1 rectangular container worth, approximately
 9½ x 7½ x 1²/₃ inches (24 x 20 x 3.5 cm)

2½ teaspoons (8 g) unflavored gelatin
   powder
3 tablespoons water
2 large or 3 small mangoes
1 cup (240 ml) plus 3 tablespoons
   whole milk
⅓ cup (100 ml) heavy cream
3 tablespoons honey
3 tablespoons condensed milk
Cinnamon, to serve

1 Mix the unflavored gelatin powder with water, and leave to soften.
2 Peel the mangoes and remove the pits. Cut up the fruit into 1 inch (3 cm) cubes. The peeled fruit should yield about 10 oz (300 g). Put the cubes into a blender with the milk and heavy cream, and process until smooth. Strain the liquid through a fine-meshed sieve.

3 Put the strained liquid into a pan over medium heat. Turn off the heat when small bubbles form on the surface. Add the softened gelatin and 3 tablespoons honey, and mix until dissolved. Cool the pan by putting the bottom in a large bowl of ice water. Mix until the liquid has cooled to room temperature.
4 Transfer the mixture to a container. Refrigerate for at least 2 hours until set. Spoon onto plates. Combine 3 tablespoons of condensed milk and 3 tablespoons whole milk, and pour the mixture over the pudding. Sprinkle with cinnamon and serve.

Tofu Pudding Douhua

This pudding of soft-set soy milk topped with syrup is a classic Taiwanese dessert.
There's a custom in Taiwan to eat a warm version of *douhua* for breakfast.

**Makes 1 8-inch (20-cm) diameter
  bowl worth**

⅔ cup (80 g) peanuts
1½ teaspoons (5 g) of unflavored gelatin
  powder
2 tablespoons water
1¼ cups (300 ml) unsweetened soy milk
2 teaspoons cornstarch

Syrup
1-inch piece of unpeeled ginger
6 tablespoons white sugar
1⅔ cups (400 ml) water

1 Soak the peanuts in enough water to cover overnight.
2 Drain the soaked peanuts and discard the soaking water. Put the
peanuts in a pan with a generous amount of fresh water, and heat
over medium until it comes to a boil. Turn the heat down to low,
and simmer until the peanuts are soft, about 20 minutes.
3 Mix the unflavored gelatin powder with 2 tablespoons water,
and leave to soften.
4 Put the unsweetened soy milk in a pan over medium heat. Turn
off the heat when small bubbles form on the surface. Add the
softened gelatin and the cornstarch and mix to dissolve. Transfer
to a bowl and refrigerate for about 2 hours until set.
5 Put the ginger, sugar and 1⅔ cups (400 ml) water in a pan, and
heat over medium. When it comes to a boil skim the surface, turn
the heat down to low, and simmer for about 15 minutes. Leave to
cool to room temperature, then chill in the refrigerator.
6 Spoon the pudding into serving bowls. Top with the boiled
peanuts, and pour the Syrup over all.

Cilantro and Coconut Ice Cream

Fresh cilantro (coriander leaves) with coconut milk is a very Vietnamese flavor. Subtly sweet, it's hard to stop eating this delicious ice cream.

Makes 1 rectangular container worth, approximately 9½ x 7¾ x 1⅔ inches (24 x 20 x 3.5 cm)

10 bunches cilantro (coriander), roots intact
¾ cup (200 ml) coconut milk
¾ cup (200 ml) unsweetened soy milk
⅔ cup (75 g) white sugar
Pinch of salt

1 Wash the cilantro/coriander. Chop the roots finely, and chop the leaves roughly.
2 Put the cilantro, coconut milk, unsweetened soy milk, sugar and a pinch of salt into a food blender. Process until smooth. Transfer the mixture to a container, and freeze for about 1 hour.
3 Take the container out and stir the mixture with a fork. Freeze for another hour. Repeat one more time. Break up the ice cream into easy-to-eat pieces, transfer to serving bowls, and sprinkle on some coarsely ground black pepper.

Custard Pudding Banh Flan

A rich dessert, due to the condensed milk in it, the caramel matches well with the velvety pudding.

Makes 6 2⅔ oz (80 g) cups

3 eggs plus 1 egg yolk
1¼ cups (300 ml) whole milk
⅓ cup (80 ml) condensed milk
Ice cubes, to serve
Mint leaves, to serve

Syrup
½ cup (100 g) granulated sugar
1 tablespoon water
¼ cup (50 ml) espresso

1 Put the 3 eggs, the egg yolk, milk and condensed milk in a bowl. Mix well with a whisk, then strain through a fine mesh sieve.
2 Put the granulated sugar and water in a small pan and heat over medium. Cook while stirring constantly until it turns a caramel color.
3 Turn off the heat, and cool the bottom of the pan by putting it briefly on a moistened and wrung-out kitchen towel. Add the espresso to the pan (be careful of splattering) and mix. Distribute the Syrup while it's still hot into 6 pudding cups.
4 When the caramel Syrup is cool, pour the pudding mixture into the cups. Burst any bubbles by poking them with a skewer or scooping them off with a spoon.
5 Fill a steamer with water and bring to a boil. Put in the pudding cups when the steam is rising. Steam over medium-low heat for about 5 minutes, then turn the heat to low and steam for another 12 minutes or so. When a skewer inserted into one comes out clean, take the cups out of the steamer and cool to room temperature. Chill in the refrigerator.
6 Run a knife around the edge of the puddings, invert onto serving plates, and add a few ice cubes and some mint leaves.

Cilantro Cookies

These coriander cookies are popular as a gift to bring home from Vietnam. The thin, crispy texture is very addictive.

Makes 16 2 x 1 inch (5 x 2.5cm) rectangular cookies

1 cup (100g) cake flour
¼ cup (50g) white sugar
3 to 4 tablespoons coconut or soy milk
3 tablespoons peanut butter
4 sprigs cilantro (coriander leaves) and leaves for garnish

1 Sift the flour into a bowl. Mix in the sugar, and add the coconut or soy milk. Add it little by little until the dough forms a mass that doesn't stick to your hands.
2 Place the dough on a 10 inch (25 cm) square piece of kitchen parchment paper. Put another piece of kitchen parchment on top of the dough, and roll it out over the paper until it's about 8 inches (20 cm) square.
3 Remove the paper on top of the dough (keep it for the next step), and spread peanut butter evenly over the surface of the dough. Roughly chop the cilantro and scatter evenly over the peanut butter.
4 Fold the dough over in half. Place the removed piece of kitchen parchment paper on top of the dough, and roll the dough out until it is about ¼ to ⅓ inch (7-8 mm) thick. Remove the paper and scatter the reserved cilantro leaves on the dough.
5 Preheat the oven to 350°F (180°C). Bake the dough for 15 to 20 minutes until lightly browned. Cut into 16 pieces while still warm, and cool on a rack.

Banana Coconut Fritters

Deep-fried banana fritters are soft, creamy and so delicious! The key is to sprinkle the fritters with chili pepper powder to add some spice.

Makes 2 servings

2 bananas
1 tablespoon cake flour
Vegetable and coconut oils, for frying
Chili pepper powder, to taste

Batter
1 egg
3 tablespoons coconut or soymilk
2 tablespoons cake flour

1 Cut 2 bananas in half lengthwise, and cut each piece in half in the middle. Dust with 1 tablespoon cake flour.
2 Mix 1 egg, 3 tablespoons coconut milk or soymilk and 2 tablespoons cake flour together in a bowl to make the Batter. Dip the banana pieces in the Batter.
3 Add 1 tablespoon of coconut oil to enough vegetable oil to fry the fritters. Heat the oil to 340°F (170°C), and fry the fritters until golden brown, about 90 seconds.
4 Transfer the fritters to a serving plate and sprinkle with 4 tablespoons finely shredded coconut. Sprinkle on red chili pepper powder to taste.

Cantonese Steamed Sponge Cake Ma Lai Go

This is a very moist, fluffy Chinese sponge cake. I've added the fragrance of coconut to give this a Southeast Asian twist.

Makes a 6-inch (15-cm) cake

1 cup (120 g) cake flour
½ cup (80 g) dark brown sugar
2 teaspoons baking powder
Pinch of salt
3 eggs
2 tablespoons coconut milk
4 tablespoons coconut oil

1 Combine the cake flour, dark brown sugar, baking powder and a pinch of salt, and sift together into a bowl.
2 Combine eggs, coconut milk and coconut oil in another bowl, and mix well with a whisk. Add this liquid to the flour-sugar mix and combine rapidly until smooth.
3 Line an ovenproof cake tin or bowl with kitchen parchment paper and pour in the batter.
4 Fill a steamer with water and bring to a boil. Put the tin or bowl in the steamer when the steam is rising, and cook over high heat for about 30 minutes.

Peanut and Sesame Dumplings

These dumplings are made with *shiratama* flour, a mixture of mochi rice flour and potato starch that's widely available in Japan. You can find it in Japanese grocery stores. The dumplings are so light, crispy and delicious!

Serves 2

4 tablespoons unsalted peanuts
4 tablespoons powdered sugar
4 tablespoons black sesame seeds
Vegetable oil, for frying

Dough
1 cup (100 g) *shiratama* flour, or rice flour with 1 tablespoon of cornstarch
⅓ cup (80 ml) water

1 Roughly grind the peanuts with a mortar and pestle. Add 2 tablespoons of the powdered sugar and mix. Combine the sesame seeds with the remaining powdered sugar in a separate bowl.
2 Combine the *shiratama* flour and the water in another bowl, and mix until it forms the smooth soft Dough. Add a little more water, if needed. Divide the Dough into 12 portions and form each into a ball.
3 Heat some vegetable oil to 340°F (170°C), and put in the dumplings. Deep fry until the surface starts to pop. Divide the fried dumplings into two portions, and coat one with the peanuts and the other with the sesame seeds. Arrange in serving bowl.

Dragonfruit in Jasmine Tea Syrup

Dragonfruit is marinated in a fragrant jasmine tea syrup in this simple dessert.

Makes 2 servings

4 tablespoons of jasmine tea
2 cups plus 2 tablespoons (500 ml) water
¾ cup (180 g) white sugar
1 tablespoon lemon juice and 4 lemon slices
2 dragonfruit

1 Put the tea, water and sugar in a small pan over medium heat.
2 When the pan comes to a boil, turn the heat down to low and simmer for about 3 minutes. Strain the contents through a fine-meshed sieve and cool to room temperature. Add 1 tablespoon of lemon juice and 4 lemon slices.
3 Peel 2 dragonfruit and cut into 1 inch (3 cm) cubes. Add to the syrup, and refrigerate for about 2 hours. Transfer to serving bowls.

Almond Jelly Annin Tofu

This is the quintessential Chinese dessert. This is an authentic version using bitter almonds.

Makes 1 rectangular container worth, approximately 9½ x 7¾ x 1²⁄₃ inches (24 x 20 x 3.5 cm)

15 bitter almonds
⅓ cup (80 g) plus 2 tablespoons white sugar
2²⁄₃ cups (625 ml) water
2 tablespoons dried wolfberries or goji berries
1 tablespoon kirsch (optional)
1 teaspoon (2 g) kanten or agar powder
1 cup (220 ml) whole milk

1 Soak the bitter almonds in plenty of water overnight to soften.
2 Put ⅓ cup of the sugar, 1²⁄₃ cups water and the dried wolfberries or goji berries in a small pan over medium heat. Bring to a boil, turn the heat down to low, and simmer for about 5 minutes. Turn off the heat and, if you're using kirsch, add it in. Cool to room temperature, and refrigerate.
3 Drain the bitter almonds and discard the soaking water. Put them in a blender with 1 cup of water, and process until very finely chopped. Pass the liquid through a fine-meshed sieve to strain out the bits of bitter almond.
4 Put the strained bitter almond liquid and the *kanten* or agar powder in a pan, and heat over medium. Bring to a boil while stirring to dissolve.
5 Add the milk and 2 tablespoons of the sugar to the pan, and raise the heat to medium-high. When small bubbles start to form on top of the liquid, turn the heat off.
6 Put the bottom of the pan in a large bowl of ice water to cool the contents. Transfer the liquid to a container, and refrigerate for about an hour until set. Slice into diamond-shaped pieces, transfer to serving bowls and pour in the syrup.

Published by Tuttle Publishing, an imprint of Periplus Editions (HK) Ltd.

www.tuttlepublishing.com

Original Japanese title: Asia No Men
Copyright © 2018 Maki Watanabe
English translation rights arranged with
SHUFU-TO-SEIKATSUSHA, LTD through Japan UNI Agency, Inc., Tokyo

ISBN 978-0-8048-5216-6

Original Japanese edition
Art Direction and Design Chisa Torisawa (sunshine bird graphics)
Photography Taro Terasawa
Styling Kanako Sasaki
Proofreading Soryu Co. Ltd.
Reporting and Coordination Asako Kusayanagi
Editor Noriko Tomaride
Publisher Tomoyuki Nagata

DISTRIBUTED BY

North America, Latin America & Europe
Tuttle Publishing
364 Innovation Drive
North Clarendon, VT 05759-9436 U.S.A.
Tel: (802) 773-8930
Fax: (802) 773-6993
info@tuttlepublishing.com
www.tuttlepublishing.com

Asia Pacific
Berkeley Books Pte. Ltd.
3 Kallang Sector
#04-01, Singapore 349278
Tel: (65) 6741-2178
Fax: (65) 6741-2179
inquiries@periplus.com.sg
www.tuttlepublishing.com

Printed in China   2206EP

25 24 23 22   10 9 8 7 6 5 4 3 2

"Books to Span the East and West"

Tuttle Publishing was founded in 1832 in the small New England town of Rutland, Vermont [USA]. Our core values remain as strong today as they were then—to publish best-in-class books which bring people together one page at a time. In 1948, we established a publishing office in Japan—and Tuttle is now a leader in publishing English-language books about the arts, languages and cultures of Asia. The world has become a much smaller place today and Asia's economic and cultural influence has grown. Yet the need for meaningful dialogue and information about this diverse region has never been greater. Over the past seven decades, Tuttle has published thousands of books on subjects ranging from martial arts and paper crafts to language learning and literature—and our talented authors, illustrators, designers and photographers have won many prestigious awards. We welcome you to explore the wealth of information available on Asia at **www.tuttlepublishing.com**.

Wow, looks delicious!